EVER TO EXCEL

An Illustrated History of the University of St Andrews

NORMAN H. REID

EVER TO EXCEL

An Illustrated History of the University of St Andrews

Dundee University Press
in association with

University of
St Andrews

The University of St Andrews

First published in 2011 by Dundee University Press
University of Dundee
Dundee DD1 4HN
http://www.dup.dundee.ac.uk/
in association with The University of St Andrews

Copyright © Norman H. Reid 2011

ISBN: 978 1 84586 059 2

British Library Cataloguing-in-Publication Data
A catalogue record for this book is available on request from the British Library

Typeset and designed by Teresa Monachino
Printed and bound in Britain by Butler, Tanner & Dennis, Frome, Somerset

Ever to Excel

αἰὲν ἀριστεύειν

Ἱππόλοχος δέ μ' ἔτικτε, καὶ ἐκ τοῦ φημι γενέσθαι·
πέμπε δέ μ' ἐς Τροίην, καί μοι μάλα πόλλ' ἐπέτελλεν
αἰὲν ἀριστεύειν καὶ ὑπείροχον ἔμμεναι ἄλλων,
μηδὲ γένος πατέρων αἰσχυνέμεν, οἳ μέγ' ἄριστοι
ἔν τ' Ἐφύρῃ ἐγένοντο καὶ ἐν Λυκίῃ εὐρείῃ.
ταύτης τοι γενεῆς τε καὶ αἵματος εὔχομαι εἶναι.

Hippolocus begat me. I claim to be his son, and he sent me to Troy with strict instructions: Ever to excel, to do better than others, and to bring glory to my fore-bears, who were the noblest in Ephyra and in all Lycia. This is my ancestry; this is the blood I am proud to inherit.

Homer, *Iliad*, vi, 206–11

Although the University's motto was not officially part of its heraldry until the arms shown were matriculated in 2006, it has been in use for centuries. In 1773 this plaque, still to be seen in the King James Library in South Street, was installed in Parliament Hall.

A map of St Andrews drawn by John Geddy, c.1580.
[Reproduced by permission of the Trustees of the National Library of Scotland, MS.20996]

Contents

Foreword by Professor Louise Richardson,
Principal and Vice-Chancellor of the University of St Andrews   9

Preface   10

1   Right out of the blue   12

2   Foundation and festivity   26

3   Roots of reform   50

4   Turmoil and triumph   72

5   Adversity and endurance   92

6   Beyond recognition   118

7   Conflict and growth   144

8   A bullseye centred at the outer reaches   166

Notes on sources   188
Index   199

Foreword

I am delighted to have been asked to write a Foreword to a new illustrated history of the University of St Andrews. This book, commissioned as part of our 600th anniversary celebrations, offers its readers a lively and engaging account of an institution which, from its earliest beginnings, has always stood apart from others, and not only on account of its remote geographical location in a wind-swept corner of Fife.

Since our earliest days, we have been outward-looking, cosmopolitan, and a centre for rigorous intellectual exploration and the pursuit of knowledge. Even the inevitable reversals of fortunes that followed in the wake of religious and political upheaval never managed to shake the confidence of our students and scholars in the essential importance of the study and research being undertaken here. We often talk today about the transformative power of education. In *Ever to Excel*, we gain a new insight into the role the University has played across the centuries and in all areas of society on local, national and international stages. On a more human scale, we catch enthralling glimpses of the lives of those upon whose shoulders our University still stands.

Norman Reid wears his scholarship lightly, with the result that while each and every page bears eloquent witness to the depth of his knowledge, the reader is spared abstruse passages, and complex asides. It is thanks to the clarity of his writing and the confidence with which a weight of historical material is handled that the myriad twists and turns of the University's complicated story unravel effortlessly before us.

When the six Papal Bulls of foundation arrived in St Andrews in 1413, the University organised bonfires in the streets. While no doubt marvellous to behold, I am glad that, in the publication of this book, we will have a more lasting, and quite fitting, legacy from our 600th anniversary celebrations.

Professor Louise Richardson
Principal and Vice-Chancellor of the University of St Andrews

Preface

When the late Ronald Cant wrote the introduction to *The University of St Andrews – A Short History* in 1945, he lamented that no full-scale history of the University had yet been written. It is remarkable that, although all of the 'ancient' Scottish universities that followed St Andrews had by then been subject to more or less comprehensive historical study, St Andrews, the first amongst them, had been neglected. Cant realised, however, the complexity of the task which faced anyone who took up the challenge, and perhaps he would have been unsurprised that sixty-five years later the task still lay unaccomplished. In recent years much detailed work has been undertaken by a number of talented research students under the umbrella of the 'The History of the Universities Project' project. Partly this been made possible by an acceleration of the systematic and highly professional work on the University's rich archival holdings which has been under way for some decades. It is hoped that within the aegis of the University's 600th anniversary, publication of that research will significantly increase scholarly interpretation of the fascinating and often enigmatic story of Scotland's first university.

Although its origins also lie in the enthusiasm of celebrating the 600th anniversary, the present work cannot claim such lofty ideals. Quite deliberately, this is not a serious, full-scale, academic history of the institution. Neither does it aim to supersede or to compete with Cant's work, still happily in print in its fourth edition. The intention of this book is to fill a different gap in our literature: a readable survey of the University's development in a form which will be attractive to students, alumni and friends of the University, as well as to a more general public. In particular, the institution is placed in the context of the local, national and international trends and events which shaped it, and sometimes were shaped by it. *Ever to Excel* offers a very broad-brush approach and, in the interests of both brevity and continuity, necessarily omits many of the tales, traditions and personalities which are already familiar to many who know and love the University. It would not be appropriate in a work of this type to clutter the text with footnotes and references, but at the end a note regarding sources provides information for those who wish to dig deeper.

A book of this nature is necessarily a collaborative effort, and I am indebted to many friends and colleagues who have assisted in its production. Rachel Hart, the University's Muniments Archivist, has been an invaluable source of information and advice, and has provided many insights into both sources and interpretation. Robert Crawford, Elizabeth Henderson, Roger Mason, Niall Scott, Lis Smith and Isla Woodman have also read the text and have offered further information and helpful suggestions. Statistical research assistance has been supplied by Laura Watson, Paul Churchill and Chris Hancock, and further helpful information was provided by Dundee University Archives. Pam Cranston, Jane Campbell, Maia Sheridan, Lesley Lind, Rhona Rutherford, Helen Rawson and Kevin Knox have all assisted with identifying and obtaining images, and Marc Boulay has worked his photographic wizardry for many of the illustrations. Professor Richardson has provided an excellent Foreword.

That the book appears at all is due in no small part to the support and enthusiasm of Stephen Magee, the University's Vice-Principal for External Relations. Jon Purcell and Jeremy Upton, successively Director and Acting Director of Library Services, and all of my colleagues in the library's Special Collections Department, have shown great understanding of the hours which could otherwise have been spent on library duties.

In the light of the events described in Chapter 7 there is perhaps a gentle irony in the fact that that this book is published by Dundee University Press. It is, however, quite properly symbolic of a new spirit of collaboration between the institutions which was apparently too often missing when they had a much closer constitutional relationship. John Tuckwell initiated the project before his retirement, and subsequently Hugh Andrew, Anna Day (amongst whose qualities must undoubtedly be counted patience) and the rest of the team at DUP as well as Mairi Sutherland and her colleagues at Birlinn, and the designer, Teresa Monachino, have been consistently helpful throughout its lengthy incubation.

Robert Crawford's poem 'St Andrews' from his *Selected Poems* (Cape, 2005) is reprinted by permission of the Random House Group Ltd, and of Robert himself. Other quotations are acknowledged in the Notes on Sources. Many of the illustrations in the book are from items held within the collections of the University Library. These are not individually acknowledged, although reference numbers are supplied, where appropriate. Similarly, unless otherwise credited the modern colour photography has been supplied by the Publications team within the University's Print and Design Unit, mostly taken by Peter Adamson or Rhona Rutherford. Photographs supplied by other institutions or individuals are individually credited.

My greatest debt is to my wife, Elspeth, and my younger son, Alasdair. Their willingness to forfeit valued family time has made this work possible, and Elspeth's skilled and painstaking editing of the text is responsible for much of what is good in it.

To all of the above I offer my sincere thanks. No doubt errors and infelicities remain; these, and the opinions expressed, are my own responsibility entirely.

Norman H. Reid, St Andrews
October 2010

1

Right out of the blue

St Andrews

I love how it comes right out of the blue
North Sea edge, sunstruck with oystercatchers.
A bullseye centred at the outer reaches,
A haar of kirks, one inch in front of beyond.

Robert Crawford

Legend tells how in the fourth century St Rule followed a divine command to bring relics of St Andrew ('three fingers of the right hand and the arm-bone that hangs down from the right shoulder, one tooth and a kneecap') to safety from Patras in Greece. He carried them to the west – 'at the world's end', 'to the islands situated in the ocean beneath the setting sun' – and there established the church which grew to be the fulcrum of Scottish religious life.

St Andrews seems indeed to come right out of the blue, at the outer reaches not only of Europe, but in one sense of Scotland itself. Even today, when travel is so easy, St Andrews is a little off the main north-south axis. The eastern tip of Fife, water-bound on three sides by the estuaries of Forth and Tay and the North Sea, is distinct enough to have its own microclimate. The number of hours of sunshine in an average year is amongst the highest on the UK mainland, though at times the fact may be called into doubt when assaulted by stinging sleet on a grey November day, or bombarded by summer hail.

Yet in the middle ages St Andrews was at the centre. It is quite probable that the early churches were established here precisely because in local terms it was already a centre of political activity, a hub of one of the Pictish kingdoms: its earlier name, Kinrimund (still used locally in its more modern corruption, Kilrymont), is derived from the Gaelic for 'head of the king's mount', referring to the headland above the modern harbour on which a religious establishment had existed since at least the early eighth century. To this day people flock to the town. It remains a favourite holiday and day-trip destination for Scots in search of sunshine, beautiful beaches and a curious, historic town centre. From all over the world visitors are drawn by its illustrious past, its prominence in the history of golf, and the fact that it is home to a distinguished university. Although no

Top right: The foundations of the church of St Mary of the Rock, on the cliff-top close to the medieval cathedral, which it pre-dates. The site may have been in use as a religious settlement from as early as the sixth century.

[Photograph by the author]

Right: The dramatic setting of the world's most famous golf course.

longer the ecclesiastical capital of the nation, the ruins of the splendid cathedral still draw pilgrims (although of a different type) from many lands. And in modern times the University remains at the very heart of Scottish, British and indeed international higher education.

In the early fifteenth century when its university was founded, St Andrews punched well above its weight. Its early importance as a royal seat no doubt rested both on the fertility of the surrounding land and on an easily defensible topography. Today, however, the town boasts a population of only around 18,000 people. In the fifteenth century that figure is unlikely to have reached 1,800. St Andrews was the fiftieth city in Europe to host the foundation of a university.

A comparison of the modern-day populations of the other forty-nine (excluding those with more than one million people), shows that St Andrews is roughly 6 per cent of their average size. It remains the smallest of the ancient university towns, and may well have been so ever since its foundation. Why found Scotland's first university here – this tiny bullseye centred at the outer reaches?

The answer can be found not only in the political, religious and cultural nature of Scotland in the early fifteenth century; but also on the larger stage of European history. It is a great mistake to be too insular in one's attitude to Scotland, or indeed its localities. Just as St Andrews has influenced, and been influenced by, the rest of Scotland, Scotland has always had its place in Europe. Before the early eighteenth-century parliamentary union with England, Scotland was a separate nation-state, and its politics, culture and economy were inextricably linked to those of the European mainland. St Andrews may be small, but throughout its history it has been outlying only in terms of physical distance.

The political map of Europe at the end of the fourteenth century looked very different from its modern counterpart. Although state-building had been going on for some centuries, it would take many more years of warfare and upheaval before boundaries settled to their familiar modern forms. For Scotland, however, there were two particular features of the European political landscape which were overwhelmingly important, and were catalysts for the founding of a university in St Andrews. The first was England's long-standing war with France, known as the Hundred Years' War (although it lasted for nearer 120 years, from 1337 to 1453), which was a continuation of sporadic warfare and dispute that had been a feature of their relationship for many years previously. The other was the Great Schism, due to which, as a result of disputed election to the papacy between 1378 and 1418, Europe was split in its allegiance to two separate popes, one based in Rome and the other mostly in Avignon.

England's war with France has to be seen against the backdrop of the previous century's often stormy relationship between Scotland and her southern neighbour. From the late thirteenth century, English kings had tried to make good their longstanding claims to overlordship of Scotland, resulting in extended periods of warfare between the kingdoms, which particularly characterised the reigns of the Scots kings Robert I ('the Bruce', 1306–29) and his son, David II (1329–71). A feature of these 'wars of independence' was the Scots' alliance with France: the 'Auld Alliance', first signed in 1295, was born out of mutual hostility to the English kingdom. The dispute between France and England, which, like so many medieval wars, had its roots in the ebb and flow of dynastic rivalries as nation-states developed and gradually defined their boundaries, was one of the great international tensions of its time. The part played by Scotland thus gave the country an influence which its relatively small size and limited economic power might not otherwise have justified.

The religious controversies of the period were not unrelated to political and military affairs. The papacy was both wealthy and politically influential, in

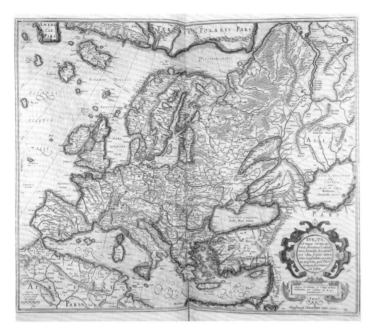

Above left: Europe, as drawn by
Gerard Mercator, and published
in his *Atlas*.

[Amsterdam, 1630; r17ff G1007.M3]

Above right: An unusual view of
King Robert the Bruce. Installed
in 1964, the statue of the king which
stands at the Battle of Bannockburn
memorial near Stirling was the work
of the sculptor Pilkington Jackson.
This photograph shows the casters
working on the bronze body of the
statue in a Cheltenham foundry.

[Photograph by J. Valentine & Co.;
JV-D8527]

effect forming a 'multinational' state in its own right. But the influence of the
papacy was not simply political: Christianity was an all-pervasive force which
bound states together in a commonality of belief and practice quite unknown
in our age. The papacy, as arbiter of the veracity of belief and the orthodoxy
of practice, wielded enormous influence within each individual state. The right
of the popes to confirm or reject senior ecclesiastical appointees, for instance,
gave them a direct political voice within the kingdoms, since these educated men
were also frequently the senior officers of state. This dual spiritual and political
role of the Church authority meant that the affairs of the kingdoms of medieval
Europe were played out both across their own boundaries and within the papal
court itself. The famous 'Declaration of Arbroath' (1320) provides a fine example.
Often cited as a Scottish 'declaration of independence', it was in fact a piece of
propagandist writing on behalf of the Scottish governing community – a letter
to Pope John XXII, asking him to use his influence to achieve a cessation of
hostilities by King Edward II of England against Robert I's Scotland. It should
be viewed against the backdrop of regular political diplomacy carried out at the
papal court involving England, Scotland and France from the 1290s onwards.
It is no surprise, then, that the Great Schism, in which countries were further
divided by their loyalty to rival popes, deepened the complexity and severity of
political turmoil within Europe.

The fortunes of both Scotland and England in the broader European scene
had a fundamental effect on the relationship between them. Whilst it is true that
Scotland's traditional trading grounds lay to the east – Scandinavia and the
Baltic, and from there west and south through the Low Countries to France –

it cannot be denied that the success of the Scots kings in satisfactorily governing their lands and managing an effective economy was heavily dependent on the maintenance of good relations with England. Local overland trade depended on peace and safe passage, and in an age when travel by sea was dangerous, there was regular travel through England to the continent. Military activity, even on a very local scale, was expensive and damaging both to the economy and to the ability to maintain law and order. A stable relationship with England was therefore important to the Scots kings, although at times it was an elusive goal. Even after the wars of independence effectively finished in 1357, conflict between the two countries remained endemic for generations to come.

When King David II died in 1371, Scotland had struggled with almost incessant warfare for over sixty years, with huge consequential damage to administrative and judicial systems, and to the economy. David II died without an heir, and the throne was therefore taken by his nephew, who ruled as King Robert II, the first of the famed Stewart royal dynasty. Already fifty-five years old when he succeeded to the throne, and deeply embroiled in the politics of the day, Robert II was not the ideal king to lead the country towards new horizons, and the internal politics of the kingdom inevitably grew more fractious. He was succeeded in 1390 by his son, Robert III, who, partially incapacitated by a kick from his horse a couple of years earlier, was no stronger a ruler. By the end of his

An illustration from the title page of a sixteenth-century guide to navigation, William Bourne's *A Regiment for the Sea*.

[London, 1577; Typ BL.B76JC]

reign, Scotland had suffered from comparatively weak rule for several decades, and was in a state of political and economic disarray. Worse was to come. Robert III's eldest son having died in the factional in-fighting of the first years of the fifteenth century, the heir to the throne was the younger son, James. When he became king on his father's death in 1406, James I was aged just twelve. Only weeks before his succession he had been captured by English pirates when on a journey to France (ostensibly for his education, but more probably for safety in a time of political instability), and spent the first eighteen years of his reign as an English prisoner. Between 1406 and 1424, therefore, Scotland remained in the grip of rule by regents.

It was into this position of political uncertainty and economic weakness that the University of St Andrews was born in 1410–11. Why now? In the midst of long-term weakness and relative poverty, the foundation of a university may not seem the most obvious priority. The answers lie in the European political and religious situation, the internal political and economic weakness of Scotland, and the position and nature of St Andrews itself.

For many years the prime destination for Scottish students had been the University of Paris. Between 1340 and 1410 around 400 Scots are known to have graduated with university degrees. Over 300 of them studied in France, with the overwhelming majority in Paris (with others at the great law

King James I of Scotland, by an unknown artist.

[By kind permission of the Scottish National Portrait Gallery. (PG 682)]

school of Orléans, and Avignon). Some had received safe conducts to study in Oxford or Cambridge, and a few had gone elsewhere in Europe, but there were well-established Scottish academic communities in Paris and Orléans in the fourteenth century. The papal schism, however, was a huge problem. Scotland, following France and opposing England (of course), had opted to offer its allegiance to the Avignon-based papacy, which caused further difficulties in the already fraught relationship with England. As the end of the first decade of the fifteenth century approached, support for the Avignon papacy of Benedict XIII was waning, reduced only to Scotland and the Spanish kingdoms of Aragon, Castille and Navarre. Benedict had been forced to move from Avignon in France to Peñiscola in his native kingdom of Aragon. Scotland was isolated.

Universities were the centres of intellectual and theological activity, which produced learned men to lead the Church. They were thus hugely influential within the discussions, negotiations and debates which characterised the efforts to heal the schism. They did not form one supra-national community of learning, however, but were themselves fractured and polarised in their attitudes to this dominant political issue of their day. The route of professional advancement was through the Church, though, and religious orthodoxy was an essential ingredient in the success and reputation of the universities. So adherents of a schismatic pope increasingly found that their welcome was waning. The traditional routes to higher education thus narrowed as the Scots found themselves increasingly isolated in their adherence to Benedict XIII. This became a crisis in 1409, when the University of Paris finally turned its back on the Avignon pope at the Council of Pisa, immediately before the University of St Andrews was established.

There was a further complication. The position of the Church in Europe had been entirely dependent on the power and authority of the papacy, and the schism inevitably inflicted huge damage on that authority. Could there be certainty that any pope was indeed the true descendent of St Peter if there was dispute regarding the authenticity of the individual's right to the position? It is hardly surprising that if this core tenet of western Christendom's belief was in doubt, then other aspects of religious authority and belief would also be subject to question. It was during the schism, therefore, that the flames of discontent with the medieval Church began to burn, and that movements towards organisational and theological reform began to take shape. The conflict between 'heresy' and 'orthodoxy' was emerging, which would lead first to persecution and eventually to Reformation both in Scotland and throughout Europe, and would figure significantly in the life of Scotland's first university.

The medieval universities of Europe were no strangers to dispute and controversy. The two major strands of philosophy which underlay the curriculum had been developed by the 'realist' school, which believed that God had ordered the world through unbreakable laws of nature that could be understood by humankind; and the 'nominalist' school, which believed that such laws would limit God's own influence, and thus that the nature and the course of universal history were less subject to human understanding. These two opposing schools of thought were at the root of frequent and deep division between and within the universities, and could affect which institutions scholars would be welcomed into. The attack on the authority of the Church, combined with the disputed fundamentals of belief and understanding, meant that the religious, philosophical and political basis of European education stood on increasingly shaky foundations. St Andrews itself would be no stranger to these intellectual controversies, even in its very early years.

A plaster cast of the skull of Pope Benedict XIII, presented to the University in 1897.

[Museum Collections, HC789; photograph by Marc Boulay]

The nature of Europe in this period actively encouraged the creation of new universities. For some centuries before the schism, the universities were truly international in nature. So institutions such as the universities of Bologna, Oxford, Cambridge and Paris served the whole of western Christendom, with communities of scholars from many countries mingling together and sharing their varied intellectual endeavours across the continent. Political configurations were changing, though. The dynastic conflicts and wars which infected medieval Europe were leading to increasing definition of national boundaries, and to political alliances and antagonisms which shaped the relationships between these emerging nation-states. In this atmosphere it made sense to provide more local educational opportunity, and the foundation of St Andrews in 1410 can thus be seen in the context of a rapid increase in the number of 'national' or local universities. Of those forty-nine European universities founded before St Andrews, more than half were established during the fourteenth or early fifteenth centuries, and St Andrews is one of no fewer than sixteen that appeared in the fifty years between 1385 and 1435. Local support for the foundation of a university is no surprise, then. Traditionally, Scotland's senior churchmen included a very high proportion of graduates, and it was increasingly the case that their knowledge, understanding and skill were required in the conduct of government. The more limited access to higher education brought about by the schism threatened the supply of university-educated men in Scotland, and there was an additional threat to the effective independent rule of the kingdom, because the king was in English captivity. Both of these factors bolstered the case for meeting the demand for higher education from within Scotland's own borders. The tendency towards isolationism and protectionism in periods of turbulence and uncertainty is not a modern phenomenon.

So, in political, intellectual and theological terms, the time was right for Scotland to take its first step into the world of higher education in the early years of the fifteenth century. That, however, does not answer the very first question – why St Andrews? The inextricable links between education and the Church in medieval times seem less obvious now, but they were crucial, and St Andrews was at the time the spiritual and organisational heart of the Scottish Church. The bishop of St Andrews was indisputably the senior bishop of Scotland and before long (1472) the see was to become the country's first archbishopric; previously, the Scottish Church had the privileged status of being a 'special daughter' of the papacy itself, owing obedience directly, without the mediation of any archbishop. The great twelfth- and thirteenth-century cathedral of St Andrews was by far the largest building of its day in Scotland, and its earlier medieval precursors had been seats of learning for centuries. Books had been copied and read in its scriptorium and library for generations. Certainly, in the twelfth and early thirteenth centuries there were bodies of 'scolares' – scholars, or pupils, perhaps students aiming towards the priesthood. The place perhaps also achieved even greater prestige when the royal house fostered the cult of St Andrew as

A philosopher teaching in Paris, from the *Grandes Chroniques de France*, 1375–9.

[By kind permission of the Bibliothèque Municipale, Castres/ Giraudon/The Bridgeman Art Library]

Scotland's 'patron saint' in the twelfth and thirteenth centuries in an attempt to bolster arguments for Scotland's ecclesiastical and political independence from England. As the seat both of Scotland's premier bishop and of a major monastic house, the town commanded a considerable landed enterprise. The possessions of the priory and diocese of St Andrews extended across much of southern and eastern Scotland, and the income raised from them placed St Andrews at the heart of a significant economic empire. The tiny town itself had grown up around the early religious establishments, and was expanded and made into a 'burgh' in the mid-twelfth century by Bishop Robert with the support of King David I.

Being a burgh gave it a status above ordinary towns, with the considerable fiscal advantages of raising revenues and holding markets. The view from the top of St Rule's tower, within the cathedral precinct, emphasises the relationship between Church and burgh: for even today the historic heart of the town retains the shape that was laid out in the twelfth century, with the three main streets, North Street, Market Street and South Street, running not quite parallel, and converging on the cathedral priory to the east. Small it may have been, but it was amongst the elite of Scottish towns, and as such played a central role in the economic life of the kingdom. Its long-standing position as a centre for pilgrimage bestowed upon it additional wealth, since its unending flow of visitors further stimulated trade.

Politically too, St Andrews was not without importance. The earls of Fife had for long been key figures in the governance of the kingdom, and for ages past they had wielded the traditional responsibility of enthroning new kings. The earldom itself was closely linked to the royal house, and Robert Stewart, earl of Fife – the younger son of King Robert II – held supreme political power in the kingdom, as governor, during long periods of incapacity of both Robert II and Robert III, and during the minority and exile of James I. The bishop of St Andrews, too, was invariably an important figure in the royal household and government, and the very close connection in these times between Church and state meant that the ecclesiastical centre of the kingdom was necessarily a place

The town of St Andrews, designed in the twelfth century to aim like an arrow at its great cathedral.

Below right: A scriptorium, such as
would have existed in St Andrews
Priory: St Andrews had been a seat
of learning for centuries before the
University was founded. From *La
treselegante delicieuse melliflue et
tresplaisante hystoire du tresnoble
victorieux et excellentissime roy
Perceforest …*

[Paris, 1528; Typ FP.B28GP, f. 2r]

Below left: The medieval seal of the
Priory of St Andrews. This copy
is attached to a document of 1566,
but the seal was in use, largely
unaltered in design, from at
least the later twelfth century.
Note the diagonal cross to the left
of the tower. In its first example,
a fragment on a document dated
c.1190 which is preserved in the
University Library, this may be
the earliest surviving use of the
'saltire' to represent St Andrew.

[Photograph by Marc Boulay,
by permission of the Keeper of the
Records of Scotland; B65/23/369]

of considerable political importance. One of the principal political figures of the early part of the wars of independence, and most important of the supporters of Robert I – King Robert the Bruce – had been William Lamberton, bishop of St Andrews. Now silent ruins, the buildings of the cathedral priory must have bustled with life when they hosted the first parliament of Robert the Bruce's reign, held in 1309 as he began to emerge victorious from Scotland's bitter civil war. Here a letter was written in the name of many Scottish nobles to King Philip IV of France, declaring their loyalty to 'the lord Robert by the grace of God king of Scotland', whom 'justice and truth and the grace of the King of Kings has raised up as our prince and leader'. It was a place with prestige. The bishop in 1410, Henry Wardlaw, was close to the royal house: he had acted as personal tutor to the young Prince James, who had lived with him in St Andrews Castle until being sent off on his ill-fated excursion to France. A graduate of Paris, Wardlaw had also studied in both Orléans and at the papal university in Avignon, and had a successful career in Scotland as advisor and diplomat in the reign of Robert III. He was an influential man, and, as we will see, was the key individual in the formal establishment of the University.

So there was political, religious, and academic purpose behind the project to found Scotland's first university. In all of those arenas, St Andrews was a profoundly appropriate location for it; in Bishop Wardlaw it had perhaps the

Right: The great medieval
cathedral of St Andrews.
Begun around 1160, the building
took almost 160 years to complete.

[Photograph by Marc Boulay]

Opposite above: The Wardlaw
coat of arms from the nineteenth-
century carved wooden screen
in St Salvator's chapel.

[Photograph by Marc Boulay]

Opposite below: The head of
the modern Rector's mace, a
gift to the University which
was first used for the installation
of Clement Freud as Rector in
2003, comprises a figure in
monk's habit representing
Lawrence of Lindores, the
University's first Rector.

[Photograph by Peter Adamson;
PGA-E1679-2]

most influential champion that the period could have produced. The only near-contemporary account of the very beginning of the University is the chronicle written by Walter Bower, abbot of the Priory of Inchcolm, an island only a few miles away in the Firth of Forth. Bower (who also provided us with the legend of St Rule) was born in 1385, and would certainly have been aware of the events of the founding of the University, perhaps even as an eye-witness. He wrote his chronicle not long afterwards, in the 1440s, and although his name has not survived in its early records, it is just possible that he was an early graduate of the University. He tells us that in May 1410 a small group of scholars came to St Andrews and took the first faltering steps towards establishing their university. He names eight scholars who began teaching in St Andrews, led by Lawrence of Lindores, who was already an internationally renowned philosopher. At least four, and very possibly all of them, had previously been educated in Paris, and it is quite possible that this was a deliberate colonisation of St Andrews by a group of scholars who, as schismatics, found themselves increasingly uncomfortable in their Parisian location. Bishop Wardlaw may have invited them to Scotland, but Bower makes no indication of this, simply stating that they arrived 'when Henry de Wardlaw was the bishop of St Andrews'. It is just as likely that if there was an invitation to them, it came to some of the others from Lawrence of Lindores, who was already in Scotland by 1408, and seems to have left Paris some time after 1403. If Lindores was indeed the instigator of the plan he would certainly have required the approval and support of the bishop, but he is unlikely to have had any difficulty gaining it. Lindores taught theology, three others (John Gill, William Croyser and – probably a little later – William Fowlis) taught logic and philosophy, and a further four (Richard Cornell, John Litstar, John Scheves and William Stephenson) taught canon law. They were all native Scots who had been educated at the great universities of Europe, and who were to develop eminent careers in both Church and state. Cornell and Lindores are the only ones who were definitely in Scotland before May 1410 (although Stephenson may have been in the country a year earlier), but whether the others arrived in a co-ordinated move or gradually, we do not know.

The arrival of the scholars cannot, however, have been an entirely random process. There must have been some degree of organisation involved. Bower says quite clearly that these men began lecturing in their subjects in May 1410: 'An institution of higher learning of university standing made a start in the city of St Andrew of Kilrymont.' If lectures were delivered, there must have been students to hear them, which implies that there must have been forward planning, organisation, and perhaps even some medieval marketing. Bower chose his words carefully, though: this was an institution 'of university standing', but it was not yet a university, which could be created only by imperial or papal authority.

Much work had yet to be done, but the foundations were there. Our little band of scholars, some of them perhaps fleeing academic persecution on the continent, had found their way to the bullseye at the outer reaches.

2

Foundation and festivity

The small group of scholars who had arrived and started teaching in St Andrews by May 1410 achieved no formal status for the best part of two years. It was not until 28 February 1412 that the bishop, Henry Wardlaw, provided a charter of incorporation, granting the scholars the 'corporate' status of a university. Unfortunately, the original document has not survived amongst the University's records; its text, however, was enshrined within the subsequent papal confirmation. The bishop's charter clearly enough recognised that until then the fledging university had been no more than a voluntary association. The charter was addressed to 'the Doctors, Masters, Bachelors and scholars' resident in St Andrews. Wardlaw claimed in the document to have originally founded the University himself, seeming to suggest that the scholars had originally come to St Andrews at least partially at his invitation.

One of the reasons he gives for formalising the foundation is that through learning and good teaching the Catholic faith could continue to flourish and be defended against the heresies which were then threatening it. Most of Wardlaw's charter, however, concerns the organisation of the University. It recognised that then, as now, town–gown relations were a subject of great importance, stating that mutual support and nourishment would be to their mutual benefit. Complex rules were laid down to govern the relationship between them. The members of the University were seen as being under the special protection of the bishop, and were to have certain privileges, such as the right to buy goods free of taxation. With these rights came responsibilities. It was the duty of the Rector of the University and of the burgh authorities to ensure that both the members of the University and the townsfolk obeyed the burgh laws and treated each other with respect. The Rector had quite significant power to punish the town authorities if they failed in this duty, and the scholars and employees of the University were given considerable financial and legal advantages over the rest of the population. The religious authorities of both priory and cathedral endorsed the charter, and endowed the University with privileges similar to those offered personally by the bishop.

The delay of almost two years in issuing this official foundation is intriguing. Wouldn't it have been more logical to found the University properly right from the start? Perhaps it suggests that the beginning had indeed been voluntary – that the scholars arrived without necessarily having the defined intention of establishing any sort of permanent institution. The charter's wording, however, makes it seem more likely that Wardlaw had been involved in the first moves, and that the idea had always been to found Scotland's first university in his cathedral city. Maybe there was no obvious need for a charter in the first days: possibly there was a 'settling-in' or experimental period, to ensure that the idea was feasible. Or it might be that the scholars found life difficult in the early days, and petitioned the bishop for the privileges which would allow the young university to survive. The charter could even have been an attempt to provide incentives for more masters and students to make their way to St Andrews, so that the University could grow larger and more viable.

Despite its charter, the University still had a problem. The bishop could offer the scholars privileges and protection, and give the institution the title of a university. He did not, though, have the authority to allow it to award degrees. It could not truly be a university without the sanction of either the pope or the Holy Roman Emperor, the descendant of the great Charlemagne. It was obviously the pope to whom Wardlaw would go to achieve this final recognition of his new university. But papal confirmation might be refused for a new university which had not proved its sustainability. Allowing it to establish itself for a while and then giving it the formality of Wardlaw's own charter of foundation provided the University with a pedigree and evidence of viability which would more likely win the support of those who governed Scotland and, of course, of the pope himself.

To approach the pope for confirmation of the foundation of a national university required the involvement of the highest authority in the land. A request, which largely recited Wardlaw's charter, was therefore duly sent off to Pope Benedict XIII at his residence in Peñiscola in Aragon, in the name of the

The faces of St Paul and of St Peter, as depicted on the seal or 'bulla' attached to the papal bull issued in the University's favour in August 1413.

[UYUY100]

king himself, the parliament (or 'Three Estates' as it was then known) and the bishop and other ecclesiastical dignitaries. Notwithstanding the fact that James I, by now aged eighteen, was still a prisoner in England, there is no doubt that he was personally involved in the planning of the whole affair. Indeed, he was regarded as one of the founders of the University: the royal emblem, the lion rampant, forms part of the institution's coat of arms. The precise date of the petition to the pope is unknown, but papal approval was given in August 1413, and took five months to reach St Andrews. Henry Ogilvie, who carried the Scots' request to the pope, must therefore have been on the road no later than March 1413, and probably considerably earlier. It is likely that both charter and petition were planned as two parts of the same process by which the University would be formally established. Benedict XIII was predictably enthusiastic. A scholar himself, he had participated in the founding or support of many universities throughout Europe. It was hardly likely, in any case, that he would have wanted to risk alienating one of the few countries which still adhered to him in those dying days of the schism.

When it came, the pope's response was splendid. No fewer than six documents (known as 'bulls', because of the lead 'bulla' or seal with which each was authenticated) were issued at Peñiscola on 28 August 1413. Received in St Andrews on 3 February 1414, they were greeted by celebrations the likes of which the town had probably never previously witnessed. Walter Bower described the scenes with glee. When they arrived,

> *a peal of all the [bells of the] city's churches was sounded. The next day, that is the following Sunday, at the ninth hour there was a formal meeting of all the clergy in the refectory (which had been specially fitted up for the occasion) when the bulls of privileges were presented to the lord bishop as chancellor of this gracious university. When the bulls had been read out before everybody, the clergy and convent processed to the high altar singing the* Te Deum laudamus *in harmonious voice. When this had been sung and everyone was on bended knee, the bishop of Ross pronounced the versicle of the Holy Spirit and the collect* Deus qui corda. *They spent the rest of this day in boundless merry-making and kept large bonfires burning in the streets and open spaces of the city while drinking wine in celebration. It was decided moreover to hold a solemn procession on the following Tuesday so as to celebrate the feast of the arrival of the privileges along with the feast of the arrival of the relics. Who can easily give an account of the character of that procession, the sweet-sounding praise of the clergy, the rejoicings of the people, the pealing of bells, the sounds of organs? On that day the prior celebrated a high mass of the Holy Spirit, the bishop of Ross preached a sermon to the clergy, and the beadle counted four hundred clergy besides lesser clerks and young monks taking part in this procession for the glory of God and the praise and honour of the [new] university, together with an astonishing crowd of people.*

The grand procession celebrating the arrival of the papal bulls in St Andrews may have resembled this procession, depicted by an anonymous fourteenth-century Italian artist.

[By kind permission of Biblioteca Augusta, Perugia/Alinari/ The Bridgeman Art Library]

It's a vibrant, perhaps eye-witness, account of the events, which gives a glowing impression of what medieval St Andrews must have been like. Bower himself may have been an austere monk, but his description of the few days' 'boundless merry-making' which marked the foundation of the University paints a picture of a society deeply imbued with religious belief and practice, but which then, as now, also enjoyed a good party. Six hundred years later, standing at the cathedral's west door, we can conjure the bells, the music for which the cathedral clergy were renowned, and the doubtless raucous celebrations of the townsfolk around the public fires which warmed them on those cold February days.

The six papal bulls authorised the establishment of the University for the reasons that had been outlined in the petition and bestowed upon it the right to confer degrees, which licensed St Andrews' graduates to teach in any university in the disciplines of Theology, Canon and Civil Law, Arts and Medicine. The bulls also confirmed and arranged for protection of the various privileges which Wardlaw and others had conferred on the University and those who would study within it. Remarkably, one of the six bulls has survived. This priceless document

Right: On 25 February 2011 HRH Prince William of Wales and Miss Catherine Middleton (then his fiancée), both alumni of St Andrews, visited the University to launch the 600th Anniversary celebrations. During the course of their visit they were shown the papal bull of 1413. The couple are pictured on that occasion, with the Principal, the Chancellor and the author.

[Photograph by Alan Richardson]

Below: The bull of Pope Benedict XIII confirming the privileges of the University of St Andrews, issued at Peñiscola on 28 August 1413.

[UYUY100]

confirmed Bishop Wardlaw's charter, and is still held by the University within its archives. The bulls had arrived just in time, for the first students had almost completed their studies, graduating only a month or two later. Their names – William Yellowlock, Stephen Kerr, Thomas Graham, Thomas Livingstone, Angus Lennox, John Homyll, Andrew McGillance, Robert Smith, John Henry, Alexander Methven and Robert Tynninghame – are still preserved in the minute book of the Faculty of Arts, which is one of the best surviving examples of this type of record from any medieval university.

The University now formally existed, but was far from what we would recognise today as a university. Following a common European model, such as at Orléans, it was in a real sense a 'community'. Masters and students together formed a corporation whose purpose was learning: all were equal members of that community. In its early days, however, it had no buildings of its own. Major meetings of the University, which was still a very small body, took place in the refectory of the priory. Smaller gatherings (such as Faculty) were held in the associated Hospital of St Leonard, close by on the site at the end of South Street

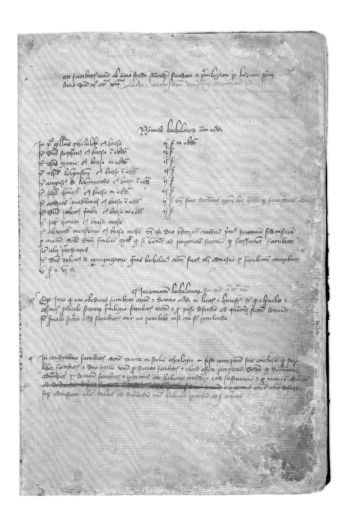

The names of the first graduates of the University, enshrined within the minute book of the Faculty of Arts.

[UYUY411, f.1r]

occupied in more modern times by St Leonard's College. At the other end of South Street, today represented by scant ruins in front of the nineteenth-century Madras College building, the church of the Dominican order, the Blackfriars, was another venue used for meetings and teaching. The students lived in the houses of townspeople or masters, and were taught in the lodgings of their masters.

Close links with the cathedral and priory were vital: the extensive priory library, for example, which had been established in the mid-twelfth century by a gift of books from its founder, Bishop Robert, provided access to texts for both masters and students. In those days, before print had made its way to Europe, books were few in number: they were scarce and precious commodities. Many of the books held by the priory were destroyed or dispersed at the Reformation in the sixteenth century, but one remarkable volume survives in the current University Library. Containing a selection of the works of St Augustine of Hippo, it was painstakingly written on vellum within the cathedral scriptorium at the end of the twelfth century. It has remained in the St Andrews area for over 800 years, and beside the more modern markings of the University Library is still to be seen the medieval ownership inscription of the priory itself. The first mention of the establishment of a library specifically for the University (or at least for

The remnant of the chapel of the Blackfriars on South Street. On this site (although not in this building, which is later), some of the early meetings of the University were held.

[Photograph by Peter Adamson; PGA6-46]

Right: The medieval seal of the
University, used to authenticate
its documents. Depicting either
students attending their master,
lit by a 'luminator' with a lamp,
or perhaps the University in
formal gathering before the
Rector, attended by the 'bedellus'
with the mace, the scene is
overshadowed by the protective
figure of St Andrew. This example
is attached to a degree parchment
awarded to Thomas James in 1626;
it was made, however, using the
original fifteenth-century brass
seal matrix which is still preserved
in the University's archive.

[Seal: UYUY348; matrix:
UYUY103]

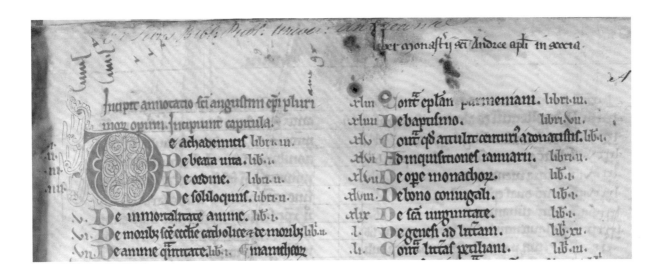

Above: The late twelfth-century
manuscript copy of the works of
St Augustine of Hippo, written in
St Andrews and preserved in the
University Library. At the top
of this, the first leaf, the words
*Liber monasterii sancti Andree
apostoli in Scocia* are the medieval
ownership inscription of the Priory
of St Andrews.

[msBR65.A9]

A page from the twelfth-century Augustine manuscript. On an impressive scale, it contains 325 vellum leaves measuring 40cm × 29cm. Each one has been beautifully and painstakingly created.

[msBR65.A9]

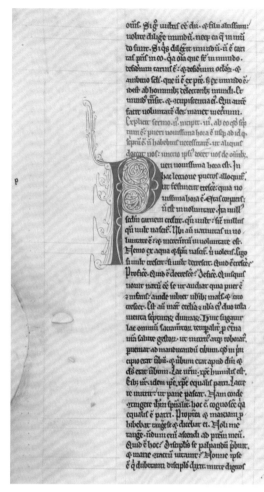

the Faculty of Arts) was in 1456, when a gift of books was given. Before then, a growing library was apparently not a top priority. As early as January 1416 the sums of £5 each were allocated to be spent on the purchase of a Faculty mace and on books. By May, however, it had been decided that the £5 for books should instead be added to the funding for the mace. Although they had occasionally done so earlier, after 1456 the masters regularly 'chose books', presumably for the library. Even then, it would have been very small, for many years probably housing no more than a few dozen volumes. Nonetheless, with its origins in the medieval priory, St Andrews University Library can reasonably claim to be the oldest continually functioning library in Scotland, and as such must be counted a national treasure.

Students did not spend hours in the library reading and writing essays. They did not even choose their courses, or sit any written examinations. Instead, perhaps literally, they sat at the feet of their masters and listened to their 'lectura' expounding on the core texts, in particular the works of Aristotle:

the standard arts curriculum demanded the study primarily of logic, rhetoric, physics, metaphysics and ethics. For those who did not already have sufficient grounding, Latin grammar was taught in a grammar school under the control of the Faculty of Arts. All the learning received by the students came from the lips of the masters: this is why the particular brand of philosophy or theology espoused by the masters was so important. Like modern undergraduates, students quickly became practised in the art of disputation, a central skill of the medieval academic; examinations were generally by oral questioning. All teaching and examining – and indeed, officially at least, casual conversation – was conducted in Latin, which remained the official language of the University until 1747.

There were three levels of attainment for early students: after a short time, usually towards the end of the first term, students were 'incorporated' into the University – the equivalent of modern matriculation, although it happened only once, rather than annually. They came to study with one master (who received payment directly from the students, not generally from the University), and were presented for incorporation by the master himself. This caused some problems. The university had to issue edicts against masters touting to 'steal' students from other masters, and several were punished for flouting these regulations. After around three years of study, a satisfactory student could 'determine', which allowed graduation with a Bachelor's degree. In the Faculty of Arts a further year's study would enable him to be 'licensed' as a Master – giving him, formally, an obligation and licence to teach. Although courses in the other 'higher' faculties of Law and Medicine were shorter, in Theology the licence required four years of study beyond the bachelorship, and a doctorate yet a further four. A full course of study in Theology could therefore easily occupy at least twelve years. Given, however, that the students frequently began their studies as young as twelve, the age at which today's children start their secondary schooling, the overall educational process was not perhaps as lengthy as it seems. Not all students saw the whole course through: many studied for a shorter time, and then moved on either to other universities or to pursue their careers.

There were celebrations involving feasts and banquets at each stage, and the students were expected to give gifts – of gloves, for example – to their masters. The presentation of gloves was no mere formality: in the 1460s, following complaints, the Faculty of Arts made rules to regulate the quality of presentation gloves. The age-old initiation rite which involved the more experienced students extorting some form of tribute from the new students or 'bejeants' – from the French *bec-jaune*, or 'fledgling' – was common throughout the European university system. The current modern St Andrean custom of 'Raisin Weekend' may have developed from these roots. First-years nowadays have to entertain and give a packet of raisins to their seniors, and they receive a receipt – often inscribed on some unlikely or unwieldy object – an event which culminates in a massive foam-fight between the members of 'academic families' in the quadrangle on Raisin Monday.

The high jinks which take place on 'Raisin Monday' in the modern University may have medieval origins in the European-wide customs associated with the initiation of new students, or 'bejeants'.

Students no doubt worked hard, for long hours, and the University appears to have been quite dictatorial. In 1453 students were forbidden to wear 'beaked shoes, round hoods or gowns open at the neck, showing gay shirts', and there are even occasional petitions for the Faculty to allow masters dispensation to wear clothes of their own choosing when outside the University. Student life has never consisted entirely of work. Records of the non-academic life of the early University are scant, but there are occasional hints. Students were supposed to take walks (in an orderly fashion, and speaking only in Latin); the time they were allowed to spend on sporting pastimes such as cock-fighting was limited; and regular feasts and celebrations punctuated the academic calendar. One of the very earliest Scottish references to performance of a May Day folk play, with its roots in ancient pagan ritual, is found in the Faculty's ordinance regarding what the students should wear at this 'Feast of Kings'. Playing football (*pilam pedalem*), however, was banned: legislation outlawed the game throughout the kingdom, since it was thought to divert the citizens from more useful pursuits, such as archery. Nonetheless, the ban was predictably unsuccessful: there are later injunctions against students who played it. In 1537 an inter-college game apparently caused a near-riot on Shrove Tuesday. Curiously, though, the Faculty accounts for that year actually reveal that the Bursar bought a football, for the quite substantial sum of eight pennies! Students would also spend some of their time on archery practice. This was not just for sport, but a legal obligation. In 1424, one of several acts passed by parliament bolstering arrangements for defence of the kingdom obliged all men to train themselves to be archers from

A fashionable young man of the late fifteenth century: note the gown open at the neck, showing a 'gay shirt' (*Beardless Young Man*, possibly Bartolomeo Liviano d'Alviano (1455–1515), by an anonymous Italian artist).

[By kind permission of the Society of Antiquaries of London/ The Bridgeman Art Library]

the age of twelve, and ordered the setting up of targets 'especially beside parish churches, where men on holy days may come and shoot at least three times and have practice of archery'. The University had its own archery competition by the early seventeenth century, and had bow butts (or targets) set up in the college grounds for regular practice. In St Andrews, as well, it can hardly be a surprise that students spent at least some of their leisure time at 'the gowff'!

The darker side of life in medieval Scotland had an impact too. Along with the rules about unacceptably fashionable clothing, the University found it necessary to issue an edict forbidding students to carry knives, large or small. This was not pointless rule-making. There were numerous academic, theological and philosophical disagreements to be sorted out by the Faculty of Arts, which sometimes boiled over into violent disputes. In 1470, for instance, several students and masters were expelled for a night-time assault, using bows and arrows, on the dean and others of the Faculty. On one occasion, following complaints about the excessive behaviour of students, the culprits were ordered to ask for mercy on bended knee, and were subjected to corporal punishment. The fact that the masters were to a considerable extent self-employed tended to exacerbate these problems. This may be one reason why the Faculty had to wield so much power over the lives of its members; and in an effort at team-building, it ordained regular feasts and festivals. To remind us that however carefully it regulated the conduct of masters and students it could not isolate itself altogether from the outside world, a sombre minute from October 1439 makes special arrangements for the continuation of teaching during a time of plague – a reference to one of the outbreaks of 'black death' that repeatedly decimated medieval Europe's population and would periodically disrupt learning in St Andrews until the mid-seventeenth century. For the following year, no records survive. Did formal meetings cease until the danger was over? Similarly, in February 1514, only a few months after the Scottish king and many of his nobles and their men had died in the disastrous defeat by the English at the battle of Flodden, the Faculty allowed extension of the normal examination schedules. It had been impossible to complete them earlier, both because of the war (which would doubtless have removed both students and masters from their academic pursuits), and because of plague within the city before Christmas.

St Andrews' organisation was modelled upon that of the French universities familiar to most of the early masters. The Chancellor – who was almost always, for over 250 years, the bishop or archbishop of St Andrews – conferred degrees and was ultimately responsible for the correct conduct of the University's business,

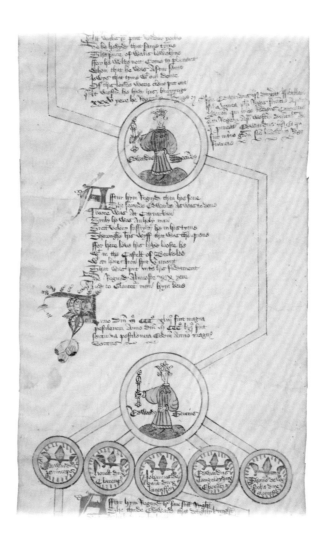

Outbreaks of plague were a common occurrence throughout the medieval period. This detail from a fifteenth-century genea-logical roll held in the University Library's manuscript collections demonstrates the ubiquity of the disease in medieval England, by depicting the 'buboes' or boils which were associated with it on the decorated 'A' beginning the sentence which tells of great outbreaks of plague (*magna pestilencia*) in 1343 and 1361.

[ms38660]

The Faculty of Arts mace. Procured in 1416, this mace is still used today for ceremonial purposes. This, and the other maces, are on display in the Museum of the University of St Andrews.

[Museum Collections]

for which purpose he might appoint a Vice-Chancellor, the executive role still held by the modern 'Principal and Vice-Chancellor'. In the medieval university, however, it was the Rector who was the key figure in the academic life of the institution, and who ruled it on a day-to-day basis. He was elected annually by all the incorporated members of the University, including the students. For voting purposes, the members were divided into four houses, or 'nations', each made up of students from a different part of the country. Each nation cast one vote, with any tie being decided by the casting vote of the outgoing Rector. At times this system resulted in dispute and turbulence, and for lengthy periods lower-ranked students were excluded from the process in the interests of public safety. The remarkable record known as the *Acta Rectorum* – the Acts of the Rectors – records the names of the students who were eligible to vote in the rectorial elections. The first Rector, who held the post frequently until his death in 1437, sometimes in conjunction with the position of Dean of the Faculty of Arts, was the philosopher Lawrence of Lindores. He had been influential in the foundation of the University, and his Europe-wide eminence must have had a profoundly beneficial effect on the status of the new University.

Academically, the University was divided into faculties. The papal bulls had named five faculties in which degrees could be awarded – Canon Law, Civil Law, Medicine, Arts and Theology. Not all of these faculties were established, though. Whilst medicine and civil law were taught at times, and although there was certainly a Faculty of Canon Law in the early days, it is not clear how well-established it was, and the Faculties of Arts and Theology were apparently the primary strengths of the University in its first centuries. Arts was traditionally regarded as a 'junior' faculty in terms of academic attainment, but at St Andrews as at many other colleges, it was the largest and most powerful of the faculties. The Dean of the Faculty of Arts was a vitally important figure in the University. Like the Rector, he was elected annually. The Faculty of Arts seems to have regarded its directives as of university-wide authority, although it must be doubted whether the other faculties would have agreed with this position. There is also no doubt that some of the violence described earlier resulted from rivalry between the Faculty and St Salvator's College, which regarded itself as largely autonomous. It is unsurprising that only the Faculty of Arts has left coherent records from the very beginnings of the University, and that its magnificent ceremonial mace, which can be seen in the modern-day Museum of the University of St Andrews, was commissioned as early as January 1416. The Faculty of Theology was slower to take shape than the Faculty of Arts. Initially it existed within the priory itself, and the prior generally acted as its dean. It was not until 1429 that it organised itself fully, and adopted a constitution very similar to that of the Faculty of Arts.

As we have already seen, the University lacked any property in the early days. This might have been one of the reasons why there were so many disputes between masters and Faculty which threatened to destroy its unity. It was not long before the problem was recognised, and efforts were made to provide central accommodation for teaching. The first step came in 1419, with a gift of land by Robert of Montrose, rector of the church of Cults (a parish some twelve miles to the west of St Andrews). The intention was to establish a College on South Street, dedicated to St John the Evangelist, for the education of students of both theology and arts. A decade or so later, Henry Wardlaw himself presented an adjoining piece of South Street land on which to accommodate the 'pedagogy', or accommodation for teaching, through which it was intended to unite the teaching facilities under one roof. For many years to come, however, the tensions between masters and the Faculty, and the disputes regarding where teaching should take place, are regular points of discussion in Faculty minutes. Although St John's College, incorporating Wardlaw's pedagogy, continued in existence within the University for a century, by the late 1520s the buildings were in such a state of decay that it ceased to function. The site was re-used later in the sixteenth century for the 'New College' of St Mary, founded in 1538.

The first enduring foundation came on 27 August 1450, when James Kennedy, the bishop of St Andrews (who had replaced Wardlaw as both bishop and Chancellor of the University following Wardlaw's death in 1440) created an entirely new college on lands in North Street. This was the College of St Salvator, whose fine collegiate church stands on the site to this day, one of the architectural treasures of the modern University. Acutely aware of the deep divisions which persisted within the Faculty of Arts, despite the attempts to centralise its teaching within the pedagogy and College of St John, Kennedy was trying to consolidate the teaching within a college which would be sufficiently well endowed to support some masters from central funds. Like the College of St John, the College of St Salvator was intended for education in both arts and theology, although the centrality of the College church to the organisation embodied the emphasis on theology in Kennedy's mind. His charter arranged for the endowment of thirteen members of the college, representing Christ (St Salvator) and the twelve apostles. In strict hierarchy, at the top was a Provost, who was to be a Doctor of Theology. He was supported by two more theology graduates – a Master and a Bachelor. They were the Principal and the Professors of the College. All three were supported by the stipends of local parishes: officially they were the rectors of those parishes, but carried out their devotional duties as Provost and canons of the College church, whilst paying for vicars to carry out their parochial duties. (This type of arrangement, whereby parishes were 'appropriated' for the support of beneficed clergy elsewhere, was very common in the pre-Reformation Church, and was to become one of the key issues targeted by the reformers.) The three were joined by four priests who had already obtained their Master of Arts degrees and were undertaking further study in theology. Lowest in the hierarchy were six poor scholars who would both study arts and be the choristers of the church.

The relationship between St Salvator's College and the rest of the University was not always an easy one. Whether it was Kennedy's founding intention

The chapel of St Salvator, the only surviving building of the original foundation of 1450. The large ranges on the north and east sides of the quadrangle are from the nineteenth century, but the quadrangle itself still occupies the site of the original college buildings.

is not clear, but the first Provost, John Athilmer, rigorously pursued a policy of autonomy for the college, and in 1469, shortly after Kennedy's death, in an attempt to exert independence, the college even obtained a grant from the papacy authorising it to award degrees independently of the University. It did not fulfil its founder's ambition of removing the causes of dispute, and indeed at times the tensions between its staff and students and those of the Faculty of Arts spilled over into violence. St Salvator's desire for autonomy and its disputatious relationship with the Faculty of Arts probably had a great deal to do with the continuing rivalry between the nominalist and realist schools of thought. Later, St Salvator's College came more closely within the fold of the University's overall authority. Known as the 'Auld College', it did stand the test of time as one of the institution's three long-standing colleges. In 1465 Kennedy himself, a life-long supporter of the foundation, was laid to rest in an impressive sarcophagus that

still lies within the walls of the church today. Church and sarcophagus alike are wonderful examples of late gothic architecture. The tomb's elaborately carved stone canopy, niches and pillars reveal the strong influence of continental design, demonstrating the ever-present internationalism of Scottish culture. In his will Kennedy also further endowed the College, and he donated to the University another of its magnificent medieval silver maces, that of St Salvator's College. No other university in the world has such a splendid collection of medieval maces.

The next collegiate foundation came almost a century after the University first came into being. Alexander Stewart, archbishop of St Andrews, a young man of considerable learning who had studied with Erasmus in Italy, at first intended to breathe new life into the old pedagogy, which by the early sixteenth century was in a state of extreme disrepair. Aged only twenty when he died at the Battle of Flodden in 1513, Stewart was an illegitimate son of King James IV. Had he lived to oversee the early life of his foundation, it might have taken a different form. However, the prior of St Andrews, John Hepburn, had grander ideas, and although in 1512 they jointly endowed the new College of St Leonard, it was Hepburn who lived to mould its development. Like St Salvator's it was a religious establishment. Attached to the priory itself, the College of St Leonard

The interior of St Salvator's chapel. An exquisite survival of Scottish late gothic architecture.

[Photograph by Peter Adamson; PGA-DVD1-34]

was intended for the education in both arts and theology of poor scholars, novices of the Augustinian order. It took its name from the old Hospital of St Leonard, a pilgrim hospice of the cathedral which had existed since at least the mid-twelfth century. It was sometimes the venue for meetings of the Faculty of Arts, and now saw new life as a university college in its own right.

The College buildings, close to and partly within the cathedral precinct, formed a courtyard of residence, teaching accommodation, common hall and chapel. The chapel, although in ruins by the later eighteenth century, was restored in the twentieth century and, on a smaller and more intimate scale than St Salvator's, is still owned by the University and remains in use today. The organisation of St Leonard's College was similar to St Salvator's, with a principal who was a canon of the priory, masters who were also chaplains, and twenty scholars. It was well endowed with lands, which gave it a long-lasting security. It too was to some extent distinct from the rest of the University, with its strong ties to the priory. Although the awarding of degrees was under the wing of the faculties, its relative autonomy in both administration and teaching paved the way for it to develop a justifiable reputation as the most radical of the University's colleges. Many eminent scholars would pass through the doors of St Leonard's College.

Below left and centre: The St Salvator's mace (centre), a gift to the College of its founder, Bishop Kennedy. It is shown alongside the other medieval mace, that of the Faculty of Canon Law, which may have been a bequest of Bishop Wardlaw to the University.

[Museum Collections]

Below right: The tomb of Archbishop Kennedy in St Salvator's chapel, in an engraving from R.W. Billings, *The Baronial and Ecclesiastical Antiquities of Scotland* (Edinburgh, [1845–52], vol. 1). Commissioned by Kennedy himself, its ornate style shows considerable continental influence.

[r DA875.B6A]

Right: St Leonard's chapel, now restored, and in use by the University.

Below: An eighteenth-century drawing of the buildings of St Leonard's College, from an album of sketches of the town by John Oliphant, dated 1767.

[Gra DA890.S106, no.14]

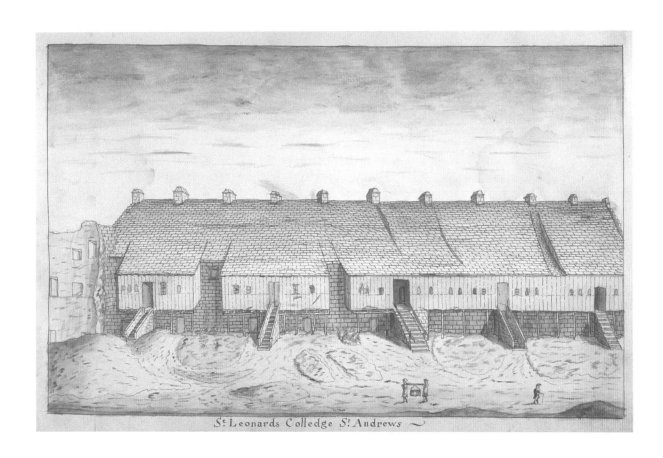

St Leonards Colledge St Andrews

A bible, printed in Rouen in 1511, with a chain still attached which was used to secure it to a lectern or shelf. Possibly bound in the Priory of St Andrews, this book is said (although without firm evidence) to be the 'foundation bible' of St Leonard's College. It was certainly in the College library, however: it is heavily annotated, and is inscribed with the names of several sixteenth-century students, as well as that of Robert Wilkie, Principal of the College from 1589 to 1611.

[Bib BS75.B11]

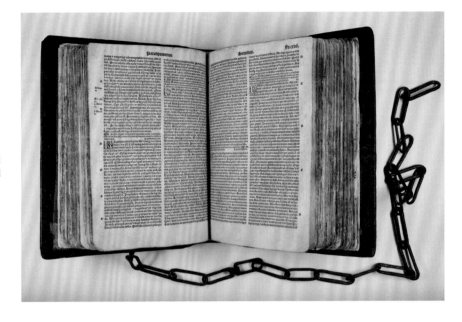

By the early sixteenth century, then, the University was taking shape at the heart of the town in North Street and South Street. There it was to remain until its westwards expansion in the twentieth century. Town and University grew together. Despite regular tensions and disputes they became increasingly interdependent. So too did the nation and the University. St Andrews came to life as a national university, and was to remain the sole seat of higher learning for almost half a century. This status obviously lent it prestige, but also exposed it to the vagaries of national and indeed international political life. As early as 1418 the University had played a key role in the international politics of the day when, finally, the papal schism was coming to an end. The cause of Benedict XIII, which had been faltering for some years, was by then hopeless; and eventually it was clear that the only way to end the damaging schism was to depose him. This was done by the Council of Constance in 1417, and it became increasingly urgent that Scotland should accept the inevitable and switch her allegiance. The young, exiled king was then represented by the 'governor' of the kingdom, his cousin, Robert Stewart, earl of Fife and duke of Albany. He was reluctant to abandon Benedict XIII, but the University took a firm lead, recognising that the restoration of peace to the fractured Church was more important than any loyalty they may have felt towards their founding father. So on 9 August 1418 the Faculty of Arts took a formal decision to withdraw support from Benedict and offer it instead to the newly elected Martin V. They sent a deputation to the governor and his council to recommend that the whole nation should follow suit. This issue was debated at a parliament held in Perth only three months later, where arguments were led by a representative of Benedict on the one side, and the University's deputation on the other. The University won the day, perhaps

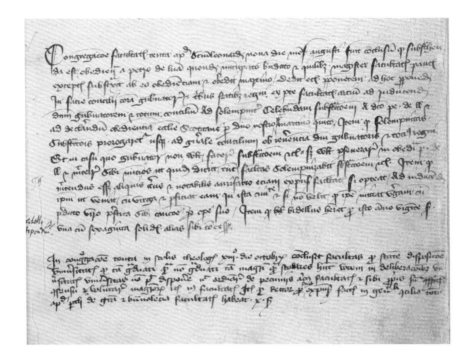

Left: The royal coat of arms on the screen in St Salvator's chapel, symbolising the close links of the early University with King James I.

[Photograph by Marc Boulay]

Right: The passage from the Faculty of Arts minutes, 9 August 1418, recording the decision to withdraw allegiance from Pope Benedict XIII, in favour of Martin V.

[UYUY411 f.4r]

Opposite: Martin V is installed as Pope at the Council of Constance, from *Chronik des Konzils von Konstanz*, by Ulrich von Richental (d.1437).

[By kind permission of a Private Collection/The Bridgeman Art Library]

bolstered by its close early association with James I himself. Finally Scotland made its contribution to the end of the schism by withdrawing its support for Benedict XIII. Papal division was to raise its head again in years to come, but for now the University had played its early part in steering the course of national foreign policy.

James I eventually returned to Scotland from his long exile in 1424, and immediately took a firm grasp of the rule of his country, which had for so long suffered from weak rule by those who governed in his name. The parliament legislated heavily in the first few years as James, who has been aptly described as 'a king unleashed', attempted to overhaul the apparatus of the state, making efforts to stabilise both the economy and law and order. One of his proposals was that he would establish the capital of his kingdom in Perth, which is relatively central within Scotland. Edinburgh, today taken for granted as the kingdom's capital, was only one of several centres used by the medieval monarchs, whose courts were itinerant. The king and his court, for instance, spent Christmas 1425 in St Andrews, no doubt as guests of the priory. In 1426 James actually went as far as sending a petition to the pope to move the University to Perth. There was a dual motive for this: it may have been convenient to have the University in the capital city but, perhaps more importantly, James was keen to reduce the influence of the Church within the government of the state.

By moving the University away from St Andrews, James planned to limit the level of control exercised by the Church, particularly by the bishop of St Andrews and Lawrence of Lindores, both of whom were highly influential figures.

Nothing came of it, but threats to the continuation of the University in St Andrews would recur. Early in 1430, perhaps in response to the earlier threat, the Faculty of Arts sent a formal deputation, carrying its authority with it in the shape of its mace, to a parliament held in Perth, to try to negotiate certain privileges. There is no parliamentary record of the discussion, so it is not clear precisely what was sought. There can be no coincidence, however, that very soon thereafter Henry Wardlaw gifted further land on South Street in an attempt to consolidate the University's teaching within the College of St John and the pedagogy: these developments may well have been pushed forward partly at the behest of the king himself. A couple of years later James I did confirm the privileges of the University, including immunity for its members from taxation – a valued concession, since taxation had made James I very unpopular. The confirmation of its privileges by one of its founders was of great importance at a time when bulls issued by Benedict XIII might have been seen as being of doubtful validity. The issue of having a single pedagogy for teaching was a complex one; confusion and dispute over this was a persistent affliction. In 1432 the king sent a personal representative to try to browbeat the Faculty into order. Changes were made to its organisation, increasing the power of the dean and attempting to foster a sense of common purpose. Clearly, the king was deeply concerned, on a personal level, to ensure that the University continued to function effectively in the national interest, no matter where it was located.

James I's interest was to be short-lived, as his reign ended abruptly with his murder in 1437. His over-energetic attempts to reform and to control had made him too many enemies, and he fell victim to a plot hatched by some of his courtiers. His successors James II (1437–60), James III (1460–88) and James IV (1488–1513) continued to be involved with the University, exerting their influence over it when necessary. Kings frequently visited St Andrews. Their presence, with the rigmarole which surrounded them, must have powerfully endorsed the importance of the University. This was an age of 'renaissance': the Stewart monarchy under James IV and V encouraged a flourishing cultural and intellectual scene. This saw the influence of the humanist thought of continental luminaries such as Erasmus and a flowering of architectural, artistic and literary activity in Scotland, and also practical encouragement for education. In 1496 an act of James IV's parliament exhorted men of substance to have their sons educated at university, especially in arts and law. The latter, although it did not survive as a separate faculty into modern times, was important enough in this early period to merit the acquisition of its own mace, another treasured survival from medieval times, which may have been a gift or bequest from Bishop Wardlaw himself.

By the end of its first century, Scotland's first university had certainly consolidated itself, undergoing significant change and development. It had grown too. Numbers vary, but in 1514, a hundred years after the first eleven students had graduated, there were nineteen determinants and twelve licentiates. Thirteen of these students were described as 'pauperes' or poor men, meaning that they would pay no fees. Even amongst the very first graduates from the University of St Andrews were two who had been allowed to graduate without fees, on condition that if their 'fortunes improved' they would repay the Faculty at a later date. It is often said that the egalitarian principles which traditionally underpin the Scottish education system had their roots in the thought and action of the sixteenth-century reformers; it is clear, however, that, in common with some other parts of Europe, they go back much further. A century after its foundation, the numbers may not look impressive, but they indicate a total student body of perhaps seventy-five, at least double its size in the early years. This should be viewed in the context of, for example, the University of Oxford, which had declined during the fifteenth century. It should also be remembered that by then St Andrews had to compete for its students with two further Scottish universities. In 1451 Scotland's second university emerged in Glasgow, the brainchild of Kennedy's friend and colleague, William Turnbull, bishop of Glasgow. It was followed by King's College, Aberdeen in 1495. Although its prestige would ensure that it continued to attract students from throughout and beyond the nation, Scotland's first university now formed part of a broader academic community.

Falkland Palace, the hunting lodge of Scottish kings, one of several examples of fine renaissance architecture under the patronage of the Stewart kings, especially James IV (1488–1513) and James V (1513–1542), in whose reigns it was built.

[Photograph by Robert Moyes Adam; RMA-H5138]

3

Roots of reform

The sixteenth-century reformation of religion was a profound upheaval in life and society; the civil and political turmoil which accompanied it transformed Scotland and much of Europe. Its far-reaching influence on Scottish society is still evident today, and can certainly stand comparison with the long-term effects of, for instance, the industrial revolution, the world wars, or the digital revolution of our own times. How people thought, how they lived their lives, and how they related to each other all changed. As the centre of the Scottish Church, St Andrews saw more than a fair share of the civil and ecclesiastical troubles which characterised much of the sixteenth century. The University, both as a primarily religious establishment and as a centre of intellectual activity, far from being isolated from these events, was at their very heart.

If religious unrest was smouldering even before the University came to life, one of Wardlaw's founding ideals had been that the University would provide a bastion of orthodoxy with which to combat the criticisms – then denounced as heretical – which were already threatening the Church in the early fifteenth century. A century later, however, the situation was very different. From their early beginnings, calls for reform of the Church had been growing steadily throughout Europe. Not stifled by the heresy trials and inquisitions, these calls gained in strength. In the first half of the sixteenth century in many places reform became a political cause as well as a sacred one, as civil factions formed around the religious controversies in an attempt to gain the political power required to force change. It is perhaps no coincidence that a figure who was to be a moving force in the foundation of the new University, its first Rector, Lawrence of Lindores, was also Scotland's first 'inquisitor of heretical deviation', and presided over the first trial for heresy in the country's history. The result of the trial was that an English priest James Resby, a follower of the renowned English reformer John Wycliffe, was put to death at Perth a couple of years before the University took shape. It was only the beginning of a long and increasingly violent struggle.

Towards the end of the century a number of minor landowners from Ayrshire and their tenants were tried for heresy. That laymen were by now embroiled in these disputes was partly because the widening access to education rendered broader swathes of society both literate and well-read in classical and humanist literature. The University thus struggled with a conflict of interest. It had been founded at least partly to protect orthodox Christian belief and practice, but

Religious persecution intensified as the Church attempted to stem the rise of heresy in the fifteenth and sixteenth centuries. Execution of those deemed to be heretics, often by burning, was not uncommon throughout Europe. This illustration, from John Foxe's *Actes and Monuments of these latter and perilous days ...* better known as the *Book of Martyrs* (London, 1641) shows the execution of George Wishart in St Andrews in 1546 (see p.57).

[r17f BR1600.F7C41, Vol. ii, p.621]

as a community of learned and intellectual men it was also a centre of debate and progressive thought in theology, culture and literature. In the late fifteenth century St Andrews was *alma mater* to two of Scotland's great 'makars' (poets), William Dunbar and Gavin Douglas, whose use of the vernacular Scottish language demonstrates a new development in learning. Their work was made available to an ever-widening circle through the technological miracle of printing. The first books printed in Scotland, under a royal licence granted to the Edinburgh printers Walter Chepman and Andrew Millar in 1507, were volumes of vernacular poetry, including works by Dunbar. In St Andrews another great intellectual figure was John Mair, who prior to arriving in 1523 had taught extensively and influentially on the continent and in Glasgow. He professed himself sceptical of humanist thought, the Renaissance movement which veered away from the study of classical writings through the medium of their medieval interpreters, and instead aimed to gain deeper understanding of the texts in their original languages. Sceptical Mair may have been, but his hugely important *History of Greater Britain*, published in 1521, was suffused with humanist leanings. Humanism and Protestantism were not unconnected, and the heretical ideas of Luther and the other continental reformers were rapidly gaining ground as the lay understanding of philosophical and theological concepts spread.

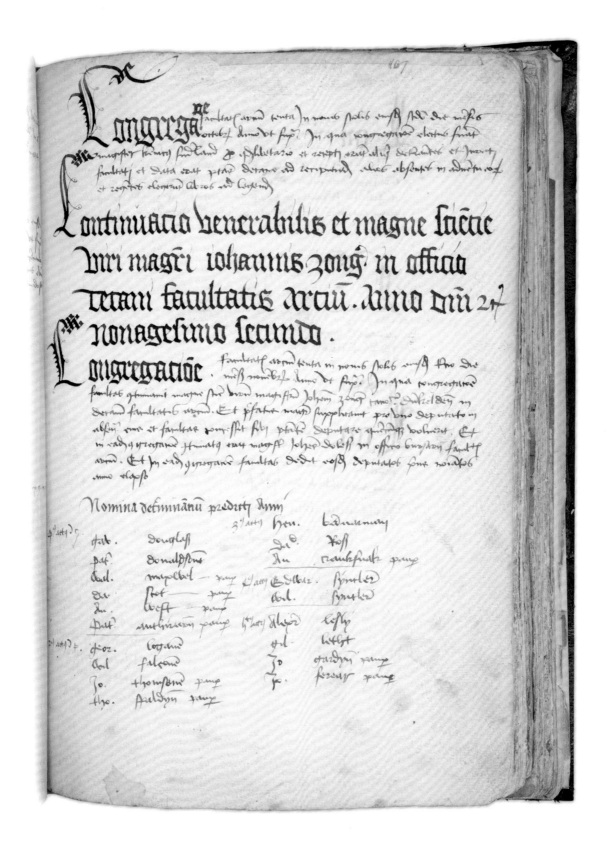

Opposite: The page of the minute book of the Faculty of Arts recording the matriculation entries for 1490, which include that of the poet Gavin Douglas (famous for his translation of the *Aeneid* into Scots). Douglas went on to have a prominent career in the Church, becoming bishop of Dunkeld.

[UYUY411 f.107r]

Right: The elaborate title page of John Mair's *In quartum sententiarum quaestiones* … (Paris, 1519). Mair was one of the great intellectuals of Europe, who taught in St Andrews during the sixteenth century.

[Typ FP.B19BM]

Whilst the older St Andrews, as might be expected, was less philosophically 'leading-edge' than the more modern and self-consciously humanist University of Aberdeen, it was far from insulated from the intellectual, theological and political turmoil of the times. This was savagely demonstrated in February 1528, when the first Scottish Protestant martyr was burned at the stake. Patrick Hamilton had studied in several continental universities, including Paris, where he may have sat at the feet of John Mair; but, unlike Mair, Hamilton adopted Lutheran thought, which in the eyes of the Church authorities made him a heretic. Arriving to teach in St Andrews in 1524, he then pursued further study on the continent, but was tried and sentenced to death a year after his return to St Andrews. The execution fire burned on North Street in front of St Salvator's tower, where a monogram set in the cobbles of the pavement still commemorates the event. Student folklore has it that to step on the monogram brings bad luck in examinations. Scotland saw fewer ecclesiastical executions than some other countries – only around twenty in the following thirty years. The event sent shockwaves through the historic walls of the town.

Against this backdrop the University saw the foundation of an additional college. Perhaps as part of an attempt to reform the old and crumbling pedagogy, Archbishop James Beaton petitioned the Pope in 1525 for permission to establish a new college in St Andrews. The foundation did not take root then, but in 1537 he tried again, with success. In the following year another papal bull was issued (and renewed a year later, in February 1539), granting the authority to establish the College of St Mary, for the teaching of theology, law, physic (medicine) and other disciplines. Planned as a college of priests and scholars living together, it quickly became clear that this was intended primarily as a theological college, for the training of priests. Its first Principal, Archibald Hay, was a noted humanist philosopher who would have intended to make effective the College's role of providing a soundly educated clergy for the Catholic Church. Although the abuses rife within the pre-Reformation Church have been highlighted often enough, it is not the case that there was no will for reform within the Church itself. Hay and others like him (no doubt including Archbishop Beaton) recognised the problems, and the very existence of St Mary's College is testament to the fact that there was genuine concern to improve the Church, whilst avoiding the wholesale theological and organisational disruption which was ultimately its fate. However, the 'New College' was formally founded only a few days before the death of Archbishop Beaton in February 1539, and within a very short space of time it would be sucked into the maelstrom of secular and religious politics that convulsed Scotland in this tumultuous period.

The monogram on North Street, below the tower of St Salvator's chapel, commemorating the spot where Patrick Hamilton was executed.

James Beaton's successor to the archbishopric was his nephew, David Beaton. He was ecclesiastically eminent: holding both his own Scottish archbishopric and a bishopric in France, he had been appointed a cardinal by Pope Paul III at the end of 1538. He was also Chancellor of the kingdom, a key political role. At the pinnacle of both political and ecclesiastical affairs, he was at the very centre of the strife which soon engulfed the country and cost him his life. King James V's marriage to the French noblewoman Marie de Guise in 1538 strengthened Scotland's links with Catholic France. It also heightened tension between Scotland and England, which, under Henry VIII (James' uncle) had recently rejected the authority of the Pope. James V, however, was not straightforward in his adherence to religious orthodoxy: whilst formally critical of the new humanist and Lutheran doctrines, which he demonstrated by occasional trials and persecutions, he nonetheless did nothing to discourage the growing anti-clericalism which characterised the movement towards reform. James used

The bull of Pope Paul III, 1538, confirming the foundation of St Mary's College.

[UYSM110/B1/P13]

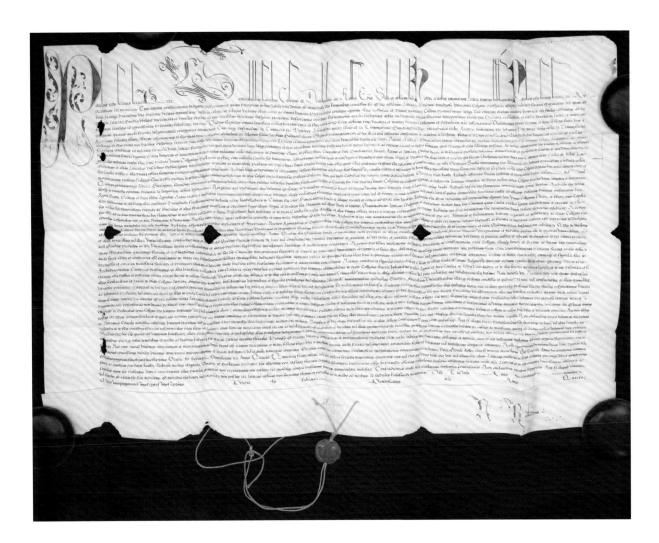

the pope's weakening position to strengthen royal control over the Church (and in particular its revenues). His early and unexpected death at the end of 1542, however, only a few days after the birth of his daughter Mary, left the kingdom in a state of profound unease and instability.

St Andrews was to play a vital role in the upheaval that was to follow. Mary, Queen of Scots, at the age of one week, represented a threat to the Protestant monarchy of Henry VIII. If Henry's divorce – illegal in Catholic eyes – made his subsequent progeny illegitimate, then Mary, Queen of Scots, the grand-daughter of his sister, was next in line to the English throne after his only legitimate child, the unmarried Mary Tudor. England and France both sought to use the young Queen of Scots to their own political ends: Henry VIII by seeking a dynastic

Martyr's Monument in S Andrews. Erected in 1842, the monument commemorates those who died in the town as a result of religious persecution leading up to the Reformation.

[Photograph by the author]

takeover of Scotland through a marriage of Mary to his own son, thus neutralising the pro-French thorn in the flesh of his northern border; and France by seeking marriage with a strategic ally in order to avoid the dynastic union of England and Scotland. What happened in Scotland following James V's death, then, was a matter of some importance.

Early in Mary's minority, power in Scotland was taken by the Earl of Arran, who was next in line to the throne should Mary fail to survive. Arran was sympathetic to the cause of religious reform, and therefore to the policy of accepting an English marriage for Mary, which was duly negotiated. He had underestimated the strength of religiously orthodox and politically anti-English feeling in the country, however; doubtless there was fear that the intention of the English king, as had apparently so often been the case, was to subject Scotland to English rule. The pro-Catholic party in Scotland, led by the Queen Mother, Marie de Guise and David Beaton, Cardinal and archbishop of St Andrews, succeeded in forcing Arran to change direction, and to cancel both the treaty with England and some pro-reform legislation which Arran had passed. Henry VIII's attempts to win the marriage by force, with a series of invasions known as the 'Rough Wooing' (in which the port city of St Andrews was a specific target of the English forces) only served to strengthen the patriotic anti-English sentiment already rife in the country, and to push Scotland back into the arms of an anti-reform agenda which saw further persecution and trials for heresy (promoted by Cardinal Beaton) taking place during the 1540s.

Echoing the shocking death of Patrick Hamilton almost two decades earlier, St Andrews again played host to the most celebrated of these trials, which led to the execution of George Wishart in March 1546. Wishart had been preaching primarily in the east coast burghs for a couple of years previously, gaining much popularity. Apparently in revenge for Wishart's death, in May of the same year a band of radical Protestant nobles broke into St Andrews Castle, the archbishop's residence, and murdered him. They are said to have hung his body from a window before throwing it onto the midden heap below. They then held the castle, which was duly laid under siege by the Scottish government under Arran, until an armistice ceased hostilities (but left the castle in the insurgents' hands) in December. The following spring a priest named John Knox, who just might have been a St Andrews graduate and who was to become one of the famous figures of the Scottish Reformation, joined the group in the castle. It is from this date that his Protestant preaching career began. Eventually, in July 1547, a French fleet came to the aid of the Scottish government, captured the castle, and exiled as galley slaves those who were not imprisoned, including Knox. Later to return, his shade lives on in St Andrews within the University mythology which claims that St Andrews graduates are 'capped' with a fragment of his trousers. The sober fact is, however, that the garment still used at graduation ceremonies is an ordinary academic cap, a 'birretum', which the University records clearly show was bought for the purpose in December 1696 from James Johnston, a St Andrews tailor.

St Andrews Castle.

[Photograph by the author]

It can hardly be imagined that, with St Andrews at the very centre of such extreme disturbance within the life of the kingdom, the University could have emerged unscathed. Patrick Hamilton was not the only academic to have been charged with heresy, and the intellectual and religious ferment, mixed with a degree of persecution and the physical danger of living in a war zone (and one which had only a few years earlier again been afflicted with plague), inevitably led to a scarcity of both staff and students. The records show that whilst in the early 1530s it could be expected that some sixty or seventy students might graduate annually, in session 1544/5, for example, that figure had dropped to less than twenty. No full meetings of the Faculty of Arts are recorded as having taken place between the end of 1544 and 1551. Indeed in 1547, while the castle was under siege only a few hundred yards away, St Salvator's College was badly damaged by fire. The chapel tower had been used as a gun emplacement by the troops attacking the castle, rendering the college a prime target. (The current chapel tower with its spire is the result of building repair undertaken in the aftermath of this conflict.) Not unreasonably, the University seems to have at least partially fled the scene; the Faculty maces and other regalia, and probably some of the masters and students, were moved out of harm's way to the archbishop's country residence at Monimail, some miles inland.

St Mary's College suffered badly in this period. Still a new foundation, it had hardly been properly established when it fell prey to the turmoil. James Beaton, its founder, died within days of the papal confirmation of the foundation. It barely existed, its buildings still incomplete, when David Beaton, its subsequent champion, met his violent end in the castle. It received a further blow when in September 1547 Archibald Hay, the Principal, lost his life in battle. He was fighting against an English army led by the 'Protector' Somerset (some eight months after the death of Henry VIII), which overcame the Scots forces at Pinkie, near Edinburgh. Hay cannot have been the only member of the University community who fell on that field.

The battle of Pinkie heightened the tension further, and ultimately pushed the Scottish government into even closer alliance with France. The Scots agreed in July 1548 to send the young queen to France, where she would marry the Dauphin, the heir to the French throne, and further military assistance from the French served to free Scotland of the remaining English garrisons. In the years that followed, French influence in the rule of Scotland increased steadily, until in 1554 Arran was replaced as governor by Marie de Guise herself. Still, however, the country was profoundly divided in its allegiances, split between orthodoxy and reform, between France and England.

It was left to the next archbishop, John Hamilton, to complete the task of establishing St Mary's College. In the early 1550s it was effectively re-founded. Under this new foundation it had a constitution not unlike that of St Salvator's. At its head was to be a group of four consisting of a Doctor, a Master and a Bachelor in Theology and a canon lawyer. Below them were eight priests, who would be students of theology, five regents (teachers) in arts who would specialise in philosophy, rhetoric and grammar, sixteen poor students of arts, and household staff. The College was endowed with revenues from several parishes within the archbishopric. A courtyard of new buildings was erected, utilising the site of the old pedagogy on South Street, along with more ground to the west. The buildings included a hall and chapel which no longer exist, but the teaching and residential facilities on the north and west sides of the site remain part of St Mary's College to this day. The education provided by the new College was indeed thorough. A modern priest needed a philosophical and theological training. To achieve that he had first to master grammar and rhetoric. The syllabus laid down for the students was therefore carefully structured and detailed; if it was effectively put into practice, it seems likely that with this new approach, the education received by students at St Mary's College would probably have bettered those in the existing colleges.

By now St Andrews had three colleges, each with its own separate foundation, organisation, funding, teaching staff and students, and with almost total overlap between the subjects taught. The University was a very different establishment

St Mary's College. The west range of St Mary's quadrangle dates largely from the sixteenth-century foundation.

from the centralised institution we know in modern times: there was no central administrative body, but rather a fairly loose federation of the colleges. The early tensions that sometimes afflicted relationships between the colleges and faculties continued, as the faculties vainly attempted to exert control over the activities and affairs of the colleges. The Chancellor and the Rector of the University did formally rule over the entire institution, but their role was more supervisory than managerial or administrative. They carried out regular 'visitations' of the colleges, but the fact that the resources with which masters were paid and students were supported came from the endowments of the colleges themselves meant that the central authority, which was largely without resource, could exercise little practical influence.

Nonetheless, there were times when the University had to speak with one voice; there was a ceremonial and political dimension to its activities, which gave power and influence to the offices of Rector and Chancellor. Without a unifying voice, who would represent the University in the corridors of power? The colleges had the authority to teach, but only the University had the right to award degrees. There was thus an interdependence of college, University and Faculty which, if at times uneasy, nonetheless served to maintain the academic standards which brought many academics of eminence on the European stage to a University which retained its ancient pre-eminence. Although it was no longer the only university in Scotland, and both Glasgow and Aberdeen were undoubtedly serious academic competitors, in the years leading towards the Reformation St Andrews still retained a distinctive position as Scotland's 'national' university.

Documents survive in the University's archives which present a vivid picture of how life in the late medieval university was lived. Now known as 'the St Leonard's Statutes', in 1544 the 'short order of life for the poor scholars, priests and regents' of St Leonard's College was prepared by the prior of St Andrews (demonstrating the still integral link between the College and the priory), in association with changes which were being made to the organisation of the college. Similar statutes regulated the lives of the St Mary's and St Salvator's college communities. The prior began the St Leonard's Statutes with a preamble commending the scriptural exhortation to an ordered life (the basis of the rules which ordered the great monastic communities of the middle ages), and which he explained were of particular importance to those of tender years, whose lack of experience might lead them to go 'headlong for lack of discipline'. The rules themselves regulated the governance of the College, its buildings and possessions, the payment and organisation of its staff, and the lifestyles of all of its inhabitants. New members were first examined in their mastery of grammar, their skill in both writing and Gregorian chant, and the uprightness of their character before being recommended to the prior himself for admission. Scholars were to be admitted only between the ages of fifteen and twenty-one – older than was allowed by the University regulations: the Faculty of Arts would regularly accept students from the age of twelve. Poor scholars were to be housed separately from others.

The routine of College life was harsh by modern standards. The community was awoken by the Hebdomadar (a role adopted by an individual for a week at a time) at 5.00 a.m. (5.30 a.m. in winter!), and their days were punctuated by religious observance. This meant a series of masses and other services, some sung in chant, and the high mass on ordinary days was to be celebrated at 6.00 a.m., so that the scholars' days would be 'more free for lessons and studies in good letters'. Regular confession, prayers for College benefactors and taking of the sacrament were all ordained. Classes began at 7.00 a.m. with a lesson, chosen by the Principal, being read by one of the masters. Other lessons were held throughout the week at times appointed by the masters themselves, and three times a week after dinner a lesson was given in grammar, verse (the art of writing Latin poetry), rhetoric or philosophy ('out of the book of Solomon'). The day ended at 9.00 p.m., after which any conversation was to be in low voices so as not to disturb sleep. There were regular college meetings regarding the discipline of the students, and further learning through 'repetitions' and 'disputations'. Logic, physics, philosophy, metaphysics and ethics, all based on the work of Aristotle, had to be studied before

Pages from the Statutes of St Leonard's College. This is the section which dictates that the students were to clean the college buildings to remove 'spiders' webs and other filth'.

[UYSL165/2]

they could proceed to the Master's degree. All conversation in the college was to be held in Latin, although this was a regulation that seems to have been at best irregularly observed; the only people formally allowed to speak any vernacular language were 'the cook and his boy'.

Breakfast was at 8.00 a.m., dinner at 11.30 a.m. and supper at 5.30 p.m. The menus (preordained amounts of bread and drink, broth or vegetables, meat or fish) were unvarying. During dinner and supper there was to be reading of scripture or other moral or historical works, and every Friday the statutes themselves were to be read aloud at dinner. The food was served by two students of the community, who themselves ate later with the cook. The students (four at a time, in a rota) cleaned the buildings every Saturday, and it was instructed that twice a year, before Easter and Christmas, 'the windows or glasses, canopies, altars and walls be cleared of spiders' webs and other filth by the diligent labours of all the students'.

Whether reading, cleaning or sleeping, students spent most of their time within the College precinct. The gates were open, however, between 5.00 a.m. and 9.00 p.m. (6.00 a.m. and 8.00 p.m. in winter). Visitors, it seems (especially female ones), were discouraged. 'No one from without, in especial no dishonest or worthless fellow, may be granted entrance without license of the Master Principal. In particular we will not have any woman set foot in our place, save the common laundress, who must be fifty years at the least, because, saith Hieronymus [Jerome], he cannot abide with God with his whole heart who is not free from the approaches of women.' Students could only leave the College buildings with good reason, with permission of the Principal, and with a companion to ensure appropriate behaviour. Within the city they were always to wear gown and hood, and for formal university events they were to go as a body, appropriately dressed. Once a week all students, accompanied by a master, were to go as a group to the links for 'honest games' (such as archery); any additional allowance of sports was to be paid for by toil in the garden or elsewhere.

A depiction of a student archer, from a medal won by Adam Murray in 1718. Archery, always encouraged as useful pastime, was a common activity amongst students from the earliest days of the University. Students who won the annual archery competition had to have a medal made, which was hung on a decorative silver arrow. The Museum of the University of St Andrews displays the entire collection.

[Museum Collections, Archery Medal 49]

Discipline was unbending. The regents of the College were to keep a watchful eye over the behaviour of the students. Truancy, idleness and indiscipline of any sort was punishable. Clothing and hairstyles were regulated (no beards), and the carrying of weapons, gambling, football and other 'dishonest' pastimes were prohibited. For minor misdemeanours, a first offence simply meant chastisement, but repetition could lead to expulsion from the college. For some crimes, however – lack of chastity, absence at night in the town, revealing the secrets of the place, for example – the penalty was instant dismissal.

We have a picture of a highly regulated life, certainly, but not one entirely devoid of pleasure or pastime. There were practical, as well as theological and moral, reasons for this regulation. It is important to remember that one effect of the federal nature of the University was that masters and students would tend to have a loyalty to college rather than to University: their lives were lived largely within the colleges, and inter-college activities were rare. There was undoubtedly rivalry, and it was an important part of the function of statutes that they limited the opportunity for students of different colleges to meet, and for rivalry to escalate into violence. Such affrays were not unknown. At the beginning of the seventeenth century one serious episode led to a firm enactment of the Privy Council in Edinburgh that the students of St Leonard's and St Salvator's Colleges were to take their exercise separately, in different locations. Equally, the issue of maintaining order within the town was a serious one. From the very beginning of the University, the relationship of town and gown was recognised as potentially difficult, and the restriction of the students from freely going about

Golf was a popular pastime from an early period: four men playing a game of golf, from a Book of Hours, or *The Golf Book* (English, c.1520–30).

[By kind permission of the British Library (© British Library Board. All Rights Reserved)/ The Bridgeman Art Library]

the town was no doubt partly in order to minimise any conflict, and to protect both communities from each other. The St Leonard's Statutes, it should be remembered, were promulgated in 1544, exactly when the disruption and warfare which characterised the political and religious problems of the period were coming to a head, at the outset of Henry VIII's 'Rough Wooing' and only two years before the burning of George Wishart. The town had already been, and before long would again be, a physical and ideological battleground. The insistence on regulating the movement of students within St Andrews was no doubt partly in the interests of protecting them in dangerous times.

Still, the existence of the statutes did not ensure complete obedience. That an occasional fracas broke out; that students misbehaved; that discipline sometimes became lax, was inevitable. It was therefore an important feature of the lives of all of the colleges that there were regular – annual or more frequent – visitations by the Rector or his deputies (in the case of St Salvator's), the prior or his nominee (in the case of St Leonard's) and a group of University and ecclesiastical officials appointed by the College Principal (St Mary's) in order to examine the state of the colleges' fabric, possessions, activities and behaviour. Such records as survive make it clear that correction was sometimes required: it was not unusual for the visitors to be critical of aspects of life within the colleges, and it is clear that the rules were intended for the governance, discipline and security of a whole college, masters and students alike.

Although somewhat curtailed and threatened, remarkably, the University survived the political and religious onslaught of the 1540s and 1550s. Under the governorship of Marie de Guise, Scotland became almost a French colony. In the 1550s, however, the political scenery was shifting. Edward VI of England (Henry VIII's successor) died in 1553, and was succeeded by his half-sister Mary Tudor, the daughter of Henry VIII and Catherine of Aragon. Mary's marriage to Philip, who became King of Spain in 1556, meant that England briefly reverted to being a Catholic country, a move which radically altered the political situation involving Scotland, England and France. Rivalry between France and Spain was extreme, and tension thus heightened across the Anglo-Scottish border. The cost of maintaining a secure border was high, and fuelled the unpopularity of the Guise regime in Scotland. This played into the hands of the many Protestant nobles who opposed the French, Catholic government. There was no rebellion at this stage, though, despite the best efforts of John Knox who, released from the galleys in 1549, had returned to England, reaching Scotland (via Geneva) in 1555. Guise was an astute politician, and pursued a policy of appeasement with the Protestant lords, refraining from the religious persecution which so often characterised the age. Knox, although accused of heresy, was not prosecuted, but returned to Geneva in 1556, where in 1558 he published his famous diatribe in opposition to female rule, 'The First Blast of the Trumpet against the Monstrous Regiment of Women'. Its title has often been popularly misinterpreted: the word 'regiment' simply meant 'rule': it was a politico-religious work, aimed specifically at denouncing the wielding of power by the Catholic Mary Tudor as well as Mary, Queen of Scots and her regent, Marie de Guise.

Increasingly, the Catholic regime governing Scotland was out of step with the growing demand for ecclesiastical reform. Senior Church offices were political appointments. Parish revenues were diverted from the local care of souls to support, for instance, university colleges and the extravagant private chapels which were built both as acts of piety and as symbols of secular status. Some senior churchmen led notoriously lavish lifestyles. The Catholic hierarchy itself recognised that these, and many other long-standing causes of widespread discontent, made it imperative that some movement towards Church reform was established. There was an attempt from within: as late as 1549 and 1552, under the leadership of John Hamilton, archbishop of St Andrews, councils of the Scottish Church passed a raft of statutes which attempted to rectify some of the more obvious causes of discontent. Hamilton's re-foundation of St Mary's

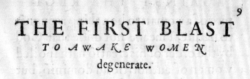

John Knox's famous *First Blast of the Trumpet against the Monstrous Regiment of Women.*

[Geneva, 1558; Mor BX9178.K6F5]

College, in the same period, must also be seen as part of this reforming agenda. In 1552 Hamilton published a vernacular catechism and defence of Catholic orthodoxy, a striking work which was intended both to combat ignorance and bolster orthodox belief amongst the clergy and their parishioners. It was the earliest book printed in St Andrews, and the first in Scotland printed outside Edinburgh. Now very rare, two copies of it survive in the University Library. The Church's own attempt at reform was half-hearted, however – too little, too late – and the government of Marie de Guise was more concerned with secular and dynastic politics.

In 1558 Mary Tudor died and was succeeded on the English throne by the Protestant Elizabeth I. A few months earlier, in accordance with the 1548 Treaty of Haddington, Mary, Queen of Scots had been married to the heir to the French throne – Francis, soon to become King of France. A magnificent poem celebrating the marriage was written by another St Andrews graduate, George

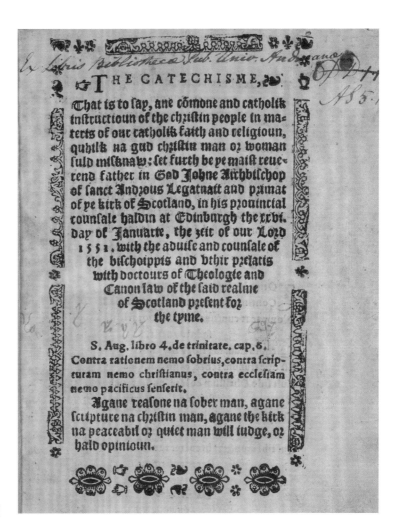

Hamilton's *Catechisme*, the first book to be published in Scotland outside Edinburgh.

[St Andrews, 1552; Typ BS.B52SH]

Buchanan, tutor to the young queen and one of the greatest poets and scholars to have studied (and later taught) in St Andrews. In Catholic eyes, Elizabeth, the daughter of Henry VIII's marriage to Anne Boleyn following his divorce of Catherine of Aragon, was illegitimate, and the legitimate heir to Mary Tudor was thus Mary, Queen of Scots, now also Queen of France. The French royal house of Valois' dynastic ambition to rule both England and France came as near as it ever did to fruition. But Mary's young husband, Francis II, was weak both mentally and physically, and instability within the government of France began to undermine the primacy of the Guise family. Scotland and St Andrews, too, played their part. A minor revolt against the regency broke out in Perth in May 1559, prompted in part by the preaching of John Knox, who had returned to Scotland. Following his earlier exile on the continent, he had spent some time in England but had alienated his natural Protestant ally, Elizabeth I, by his

This portrait of Mary Queen of Scots, published by the Dundee firm of James Valentine & Co. in 1878, demonstrates the extent to which the story of Mary was used to exemplify the romantic aspect of Scotland's past in an age which ushered in mass tourism.

[JV-88431]

fulminations against female rule. Marie de Guise obtained French military help, with the result that the opposition to her became more entrenched, and what had been a primarily religious conflict took on the mantle of a national struggle. The band of those nobles willing to bring their opposition into the open grew, and they sought assistance from Protestant England. An English army crossed the border, but events overtook it when Marie de Guise unexpectedly died in June 1560, leaving a gaping void in the government of Scotland. A political settlement was made, which included the official adoption of the Protestant faith by Scotland and which placed Lord James Stewart, Mary's half-brother, the Protestant lay prior of St Andrews and a key player in the politics of the period, at the centre of Scottish government. The French dynastic plans took a further knock when only a few months later Francis II also died, leaving Mary a young widow. No longer Queen of France, but still Queen of Scotland, she had little option but to return to Scotland, the Catholic Queen of a Protestant country. The short and increasingly disturbed and volatile reign of Mary, which came to an end in 1567–8 with her enforced abdication, flight and imprisonment in England (leading ultimately to her execution in 1587) is well enough known, and one of the great tragic tales of Scottish history. During her reign she did visit St Andrews, and it is rather doubtfully rumoured that the ancient hawthorn tree which still grows in St Mary's quadrangle was planted by her in 1563.

Lochleven castle, in which Mary Queen of Scots was imprisoned before making her escape to end up a prisoner of her cousin, Queen Elizabeth I of England, an exile which ended only with her execution in 1587.

[JV-A527]

St Andrews was still at the heart of the religious and political life of the kingdom. It would be reasonable to think that the University and its colleges, founded in order to support the established Catholic Church, had great cause to fear the Reformation, and it must have viewed the post-1560 landscape with trepidation. The reformers, however, were not unthinking revolutionaries who swept all aside. True, in common with other places, St Andrews suffered from violent destruction of the symbols of the old order: the years following

Above: George Buchanan: a portrait from the frontispiece of his *Rerum Scoticarum Historia*.

[Edinburgh, 1727; Buch DA775.B8D27]

Opposite: The ruins of St Andrews cathedral, in an engraving from R.W. Billings, *The Baronial and Ecclesiastical Antiquities of Scotland*.

[Edinburgh, (1845–52), vol. 1.; r DA875.B6A]

the Reformation saw the deliberate unroofing of the cathedral church, and the desecration of the altar and other parts of the parish church. But there was an element of pragmatic stability as well. Recognising the centrality of the universities to both civil and ecclesiastical society, the reformers had no intention of abolishing institutions which were so crucial to their plans. The *First Book of Discipline*, the reformers' manifesto for the new religious establishment, was drawn up by a committee which included two senior members of the University and at least one former student. It made quite explicit the place of the three universities in the new order, and laid out a plan for reforming each of them. In St Andrews, the reforming plan was quite conservative. It recommended that the three colleges should remain, with a realignment of the teaching specialisms to coincide with the three faculties of Law, Divinity, and Arts with Medicine. The University as a whole would continue to be presided over by an elected Rector, whose authority over the colleges (each of which had its own Principal), was more clearly defined than had previously been the case.

In fact, like many of the proposals of the *First Book of Discipline*, the plan for reform was not effectively carried out until almost two decades later, and in the meantime the University's by now rather old-fashioned lack of organisation continued. Academic standards must have varied, and the lack of defined central control presented significant dangers in terms of its finances and organisational stability. The problems were recognised, and a further scheme for reform was proposed in 1563 by a parliamentary commission (the first of many in succeeding centuries), which included George Buchanan, who was to return to St Andrews in 1566 as Principal of St Leonard's College, before becoming tutor to King James VI. One of Scotland's most famed humanist writers, Buchanan himself produced the commission's report, which proposed reforms not dissimilar to those suggested in 1560, although with a different faculty arrangement aimed at strengthening the basic education in the humanities preparatory to further studies for only a few in the 'higher' faculties of law and medicine. Again, the proposals were not put into effect, and another attempt in 1574 similarly failed. The ability of the college masters simply to plough their own furrows was too great, and successive attempts at reform were largely ignored.

The unsatisfactory nature of the University's governance, however, remained recognised, and eventually it could be ignored no longer. In the latter half of 1579 another commission was empowered to reform the University by the King and Privy Council: this time, it succeeded. In November, a 'New Foundation' of the University was confirmed by parliament. This rearrangement of the University retained the existing three colleges, maintaining the general humanities focus of St Leonard's and St Salvator's (the Principal of which was also to be Professor of Medicine) and creating out of St Mary's a college dedicated entirely to theology. The number of professors, masters and regents in different subjects was specified, and administrative and organisational arrangements were clarified. Two decades after the Reformation, we finally have a new beginning for the University.

4

Turmoil and triumph

If the medieval universities of Europe had been profoundly challenged by the upheaval of the late fifteenth and sixteenth centuries, as religious reformation turned their world upside down, it cannot be denied that they were also stimulated by it. The theological and philosophical debates which suffused the religious and political revolution were bread and butter to the academic world, and although the universities were at times used as forces of conservatism, they were also inevitably at the forefront of the new thinking. Almost without exception, the great names which resound through the ages from the Reformation in Europe – Wycliffe, Hus, Erasmus, Luther, Zwingli and Calvin, for instance – emerged from, or were connected with, the universities. If in one sense the universities suffered from periodic persecution and the disruption which followed political upheaval, in another sense they thrived on the intellectual activity which was at the heart of the conflict.

It would be easy to assume that the consistent calls for reform of the University, which culminated in the 'New Foundation' of 1579, indicate that St Andrews was an institution in decline. Certainly, there was room for improvement in the organisation and administration of the University, which was, perhaps, simply old-fashioned. Any major change in the social or economic life of a country makes new demands on its education system: in modern times regular changes to the British primary and secondary school curricula and the huge growth in the university sector, with institutions of radically different character achieving university status, are testament to the need for education to keep pace with a changing society. Sixteenth-century Scotland faced just such a challenge. The Reformation in Scotland was not a purely religious affair. In reforming the medieval Church, which had been so all-encompassing a social force, it was necessary to replace it with institutions and organisations which would fulfil the same functions, without the abuses which had been the cause of the call for reform. Thus poor relief figured prominently in the reformers' manifesto: there was little point in ensuring the religious wellbeing of the people if they could not afford to eat. Similarly, the laity could not be expected to take a significant part in the governing of the Church, or to benefit from the new forms of worship which aimed at including all, if they were not educated to at least a basic standard. Thus one of the most significant effects of the Reformation was an extension to the system of parish schooling aimed at ordinary people. It has to be doubted how

Andrew Melville, in an eighteenth-century engraving.

[GPS]

fully the reform plans, which intended to establish a school with a professional schoolmaster in every parish, were carried into effect, but the ambition and the philosophy which underpinned them were clear. It was of course equally important to the governing community that the universities also were organised in such a way as to meet the needs of post-Reformation Scotland. As in the rest of Europe, the Scottish universities could be seen as bastions of the old order, and in need of reform.

Structural reform was indeed required, but there was no sense of academic decline in this period: intellectually the University was very much alive. Some of St Andrews' most renowned alumni were here in the later sixteenth and the seventeenth centuries. A key individual in the post-Reformation period was theologian, philosopher and poet Andrew Melville. Himself a graduate of the University, with subsequent study in Paris and an already established university teaching career on the continent and in Glasgow, Melville was appointed the first Principal of the newly reformed St Mary's College in 1580. For the rest of the century he was a towering presence both in the University and indeed within the nation and beyond. Melville had taken a leading role in the reorganisation of Glasgow University in the years preceding his appointment at St Andrews, and it was clear that he had been brought to St Andrews as a reformer. With outstanding organisational abilities, he was central to the establishment of the Reformed Church in Scotland, and similarly set about the task of making changes within the College. His efforts to modernise the teaching and curriculum were not always welcome, however, and his first few years were undoubtedly troubled, with regular and serious disputes. One particular issue was Melville's insistence on changing the methodology of teaching. Under the old system of 'regenting', a student would receive his instruction, in all subjects, from one master throughout the entire duration of his four-year course. The intention of the new foundation in 1579 was to replace this method with the more effective use of 'professors' to teach within specialist subject areas. Of course, such a radical change in the way education was delivered was profoundly controversial, and it was the cause of intense friction. Although influential, Melville was certainly not always popular amongst his colleagues. In St Mary's he largely succeeded, but it was to be a century or more before the same reforms were effectively introduced to the other colleges.

For seven years from 1590 Melville was also Rector of the University, still the most powerful position within the institution. He was later accused of not having carried forward the programme of reform dictated in 1579, and was removed from the rectorship by a royal commission which visited the University in 1597. However, the undoubted effect he had on St Mary's makes it unlikely that he had not endeavoured to carry forward a similar programme in the other colleges. Indeed some reforms, such as the revision of the statutes of the faculties in an attempt to regulate the academic affairs of the University, were carried out under his leadership. It seems that his removal from office had more to do with national affairs than local or educational ones. Melville had locked horns with the king on more than one occasion, and had indeed been forced into exile for almost two years in the mid-1580s. His dispute with James VI was based on very different notions of the relationship between Church and state. Melville believed passionately in the freedom of the Church from state control, and in the submission of secular authority to the divine. James VI, however, himself no mean scholar and poet, had other ideas, and became renowned as a leading exponent of the idea of the 'divine right of kings'.

The extent to which the crown should wield authority over the national Church was an issue which caused deep division, and indeed was responsible for serious civil strife for many decades to come. In crude terms, Melville, as Principal of St Mary's theological college, saw the University as a means of bolstering the place of the Church in society; James saw the University as a means of achieving more royal control over the Church. Conflict was therefore inevitable, and on at least one occasion, in 1587, it took place in St Andrews itself in the form of discussion and argument with the king in person. From time to

Opposite: Student notes, or 'dictates' taken down from a course of lectures on 'dialectic' given by John Malcolm, a regent in St Leonard's College, c.1584–6.

[msBC59.M2]

time the disagreement flared up into serious dispute. Several commissions visited the University in this period, that of 1597 being the most radical in its effect, removing Melville from the rectorship and some other professors, his supporters, from their posts. Changes were made to ensure that no one person could be Rector for more than three years, in order to limit the hold on power of anyone of the wrong persuasion, and a new council, significantly under royal sway, was appointed to govern the institution. This arrangement was further strengthened in the royal interest by a further commission in 1599, when the earl of Montrose was appointed Chancellor of the University by the king.

In 1603 Queen Elizabeth of England died, leaving no children. James VI of Scotland, as her nearest heir, became King James I of England. He removed his court from Edinburgh to London, and ruled both kingdoms from the south. The gulf of the philosophical divide between James and Melville did not lessen, however, and eventually in 1606 Melville was accused of treason and imprisoned in the Tower of London. He was released in 1611, but lived out the rest of his life in French exile. His influence on the Scottish Church and state – and on the University of St Andrews – had been immense.

It is a curious fact that the most vibrant account that survives of life in the University in this period was a diary written by Andrew Melville's nephew James, who was a student in St Leonard's College from 1571 to 1574, and thereafter a professor in St Mary's between 1580 and 1587. He describes the commotions, disputes and political debates in fine detail, but what is outstanding about James Melville's diary is the warmth and humanity with which he describes life as a student and master within the town. The son of an Angus minister, he spent several years in local schools in and near Montrose (during the politically turbulent late 1560s), where he studied scripture, Latin and French, a formidable array of classical texts and even works by modern scholars including Erasmus, then proceeded to the University at the age of fourteen. He describes in detail his studies in the first year of his course, which he found very hard since, despite his early education, his Latin and grammar were not up to the task. With the careful help of his regent, however, he persevered and succeeded. Consistent with the earlier customs, he studied the philosophy and logic of Aristotle, as well as rhetoric, dialectic and further grammar, largely through the medium of classical writers.

The highlight of James Melville's first year, however, was the arrival of John Knox in St Andrews, who taught there for the summer and winter. Melville tells us that, listening to Knox teaching about the prophecy of Daniel, 'I had my pen and my little book, and took away such things as I could comprehend'. Knox was clearly a striking rhetorician – 'he made me so shake and tremble, that I could not hold a pen to write'. He describes how Knox gathered the masters of the College around him, and how he visited the College yard, called the students to him, and exhorted them to pursue their studies well and work for their country. The diary is also, however, an affectionate portrayal of Knox as a frail man. He was by

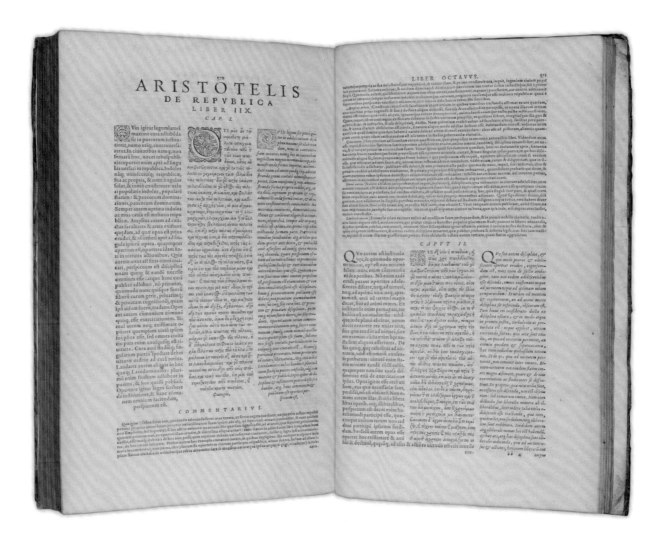

A copy of Aristotle's *Politics* published in Basel in 1582, which demonstrates the character of the humanist scholarship of the period. The central column offers the Greek text, flanked by two alternative Latin translations, and followed by extensive humanist commentaries.

[Typ SWB.B82EA]

then unwell, and died in Edinburgh in the following year, in his late fifties. In St Andrews, according to Melville, he was very weak, and went about the town slowly and cautiously with a pine-marten stole around his neck for warmth, using a stick in one hand and supported under the other arm by his servant. He had to be lifted up to the pulpit, but nonetheless managed to display such vigour in preaching 'that he seemed likely to break the pulpit into pieces and fly out of it'. Knox, charismatic to the last, clearly roused his audience: 'Our whole college, masters and scholars, were sound and zealous for the good cause; the other two colleges not so; for in the New College (St Mary's), although Mr John Douglas, then Rector, was good enough, the three other masters and some of the Regents . . . were evil minded . . . and hated Mr Knox and the good cause; . . . The old college (St Salvator's) was ruled by Mr John Rutherford, then Dean of Faculty, a man learned in philosophy, but malicious and corrupt.' Throughout this year, Melville is aware of the political events which affect and threaten his country.

Curiously, in July 1572, a play written by one of the regents, John Davidson, was performed at the wedding of one of his colleagues, 'which I saw played in Mr Knox's presence, in which . . . the castle of Edinburgh was besieged, taken, and the Captain, with one or two with him, hanged in effigy'. Appropriate nuptial celebrations!

James Melville goes on to describe his studies in subsequent years with delightful detail, such as his portrait of the 'Primarius' of the College, James Wilkie, 'a good, peaceable, sweet old man, who loved me well'. His achievement of bachelorship was celebrated 'according to the solemnities then used of Declamations, banqueting and plays'. In the later years of his course, too, Melville took some instruction in law; he boarded in the house of a lawyer, Andrew Green, who took him to the law courts, where he could see the teaching put into practice: 'but my heart was not set in that way'. He learnt music too, at the hands of the College Principal's servant, Alexander Smith, 'who had been trained up among the monks in the Abbey'. He enjoyed music, and spent time with fellow students 'fingering and playing on instruments passing well', but claims that his natural ear prevented him from learning seriously. 'It was the great mercy of God that kept me from any great progress in singing and playing on instruments, for if I had attained to any reasonable measure therein I would never have done good in other ways because of my amorous disposition.' Other pastimes included archery and golf – for which he had his bows, arrows and club and balls, but he had no money for gambling or frequenting taverns.

Given the increasing trend towards classical learning espoused by the humanist philosophers of the time, it is interesting that James Melville tells us

Below left: John Knox, in his old age. From the frontispiece of Thomas McCrie, *The Life of John Knox*.

[Edinburgh, 1840; Hay BX9223]

Below right: The interior of Holy Trinity Church, St Andrews, c.1905, shortly before extensive remodelling began. This is the church in which John Knox, in his old age, had to be lifted up to the pulpit.

[Photograph by John Fairweather; GMC-F1000]

that, other than very elementary Greek, neither Hebrew nor Greek teaching could be found. One person who had been proficient in Greek as a student was his uncle, Andrew Melville, but he was at this time abroad in Geneva, and it seems that for some years his family had no news of whether he was alive or dead. Andrew returned safely, though, and when he came to St Andrews as Principal of St Mary's in 1580, his nephew James (who came with him from Glasgow, leaving that city 'with infinite tears') describes the controversy he caused. Admitting that at the end of his course as a student he knew a little about many things, but much about nothing, James later becomes much more scathing about the education offered in the unreformed University: 'The ignorance and negligence of those who should have taught theology, meant that regents and scholars cared nothing for divinity; indeed it was even a pity to see the ignorance and profanity that was amongst them. And as for languages, arts and philosophy, they had nothing at all except a few books of Aristotle which they learnt pertinaciously to babble and dispute about, without proper understanding and use thereof.' Andrew Melville, he tells us, persuaded each of them to study languages and arts, so that they could read Aristotle in his own language, thus enabling them to become 'both philosophers and theologians, and acknowledged a wonderful transportation out of darkness into light'.

James demonstrates the zeal of the convert, of course, but nonetheless gives a flavour of the new broom sweeping clean. Disputes with the town led to threats of violence and a war of words conveyed both through the pulpit and by fixing placards and banners to the college gates (a situation which led James to fear for his life), and when Andrew Melville, in dispute with the crown, was forced to flee St Andrews temporarily in 1584/5, his nephew offers us a bleak picture of an institution in trouble, with the students threatening to scatter and classes dissolving. He did his best to keep things going, but later in 1584 was himself forced to flee, heading south by sea in a small boat to safety. Eventually returning to St Andrews in the spring of 1586 (after the towns of Scotland had started to 're-people' following a serious outbreak of plague, which had afflicted them throughout the winter months), the situation in the University, by his account, was by then fairly ruinous. His opinion is supported by the report of a royal commission in 1588, which severely criticised the state of the College finances, the disrepair of the buildings, the shortage of staff, their reluctance to adopt the professorial system of teaching, and unwarranted shortening of the teaching year. Clearly one of Andrew Melville's right-hand men in the 1580s, James left the University in 1587 to become the minister of Anstruther. His diary continues to record the religious and political events of the day (including the landing at Anstruther of a stray ship from the great, failed, Spanish Armada in 1588), and portrays his life in great detail until 1601.

The sixteenth century saw a flowering of new humanist philosophy throughout Europe, and Andrew Melville, having studied with some of its great exponents, was deeply influenced by it. Humanism's foundation was a return to the 'source' – the use of Greek and Latin classical philosophy and writings to inform current thought, as a reaction against the 'scholastic' approach, which rather filtered study through the commentaries of the great medieval writers. There was a rejection of what was seen as a corrupt medieval Latin in favour of a purist approach to writing in classical Latin. Great Scots thinkers and poets, perhaps most notably George Buchanan, were fine exponents of this trend. Poetry, rhetoric and the art of writing are hallmarks of the Renaissance humanist education. We have already seen that James Melville's education in St Leonard's in the 1570s followed this pattern to some extent, but his dismissive attitude to the quality of teaching in the University at the end of the decade indicates that, particularly in terms of language, there was much work to be done to overthrow the by now old-fashioned medieval approach. Andrew Melville's work was in conflict, therefore, both with the centralising and controlling tendencies of the crown and the episcopal organisation which it favoured, and also with the more conservative elements of the academic community itself. The later sixteenth century was thus without doubt a turbulent period in the development of the University. But despite dispute and controversy, the Melvillian and subsequent reforms did propel St Andrews into the modern era, and it is clear that many of the students who sought their education there, and the staff who taught them during the period of humanist ascendancy made very significant contributions to the life of the nation, and to learning. St Andrews, largely as a result of Melville's endeavours, became a major European centre for the study of theology.

A period of relative stability followed Andrew Melville's departure, with solid humanist academic leadership being largely subservient in administrative terms to the royalist control of successive visitations, and the presence of the archbishop of St Andrews as Vice-Chancellor (from 1599) and Chancellor (from 1605). For a while, the great religious controversies which had so afflicted the second half of the sixteenth century abated, with the Church in the hands of a 'moderate' party which saw advantage in compromise with the crown over ecclesiastical affairs. The stability helped the University, and it might even be said that although dispute was to some extent the staple fodder of academia, 'peace broke out'. In 1617, King James returned to Scotland for the first time since he had left to take the English throne in 1603. He visited St Andrews, which he enthusiastically regarded both as the centre of the Scottish Church, with the archbishop as the senior clergyman of the kingdom, and as the country's pre-eminent educational facility. His visit was thoroughly celebrated, and the king himself took part in the academic celebrations and disputations.

A very significant development of this period was the foundation of an effective central University Library. Although books had been collected since the very early days, and each college had some sort of collection to support its work, provision was at best piecemeal, and it was recognised that a 'common' library for the institution was required. Attempts had been made previously. In 1566 Mary, Queen of Scots had left a provisional legacy of books to the University for this purpose, in a will drawn up in anticipation of the perils of childbirth. In the event, however, both she and her son, the future King James VI, survived, and the bequest therefore did not come into effect. Archbishop Gledstanes, as Chancellor, actively pursued further gifts of books, and in 1612 a donation from the king himself and from other members of the royal family provided around 200 further volumes. Many of these still survive within the modern University Library in the 'Royal Collection', which also contains books gifted half a century earlier to his *alma mater*, St Leonard's College, by the earl of Moray, Regent of Scotland (the half-brother of Mary, Queen of Scots). With this increasing core of texts, accommodation was an obvious requirement. A new building was begun in 1612 on the site of the old College of St John on South Street, adjacent to St Mary's College, but financial pressures prevented its completion for many years. An instruction from the king (without funds to match!) following his visit saw it rendered wind- and water-tight in 1618, but it took a private donation more than thirty years later before it was completed and fitted out. The building provided a fine galleried library on the upper floor, with a University meeting and ceremonial hall below. Known today as 'Parliament Hall' because it housed the Scottish parliament of 1645/6, which came to St Andrews because, once again, much of the rest of Scotland was in the grip of plague, the lower hall is still at the heart of the University, used for academic and ceremonial purposes. The splendid 'King James Library' above it remains a haven for quiet study.

Below: The distinctive binding of books donated to the University Library in the 1560s by the Regent Moray. This particular book is Chrysostom, *Opera*.

[Basel, 1530; Roy BR1720.C5]

Right: The King James Library today.

[Photograph by Marc Boulay]

In the 1620s and 1630s, then, before religious and civil war once more blighted the political, social and educational landscape of both Scotland and England, St Andrews was again a favoured place. The University had increased in size quite considerably. When James Graham, earl of Montrose, later famous as the marquis of Montrose, came up to the University in session 1626/7, the records show that he was one of some sixty students matriculating, which would indicate a student population of around 250. The records are littered with the names of those who, like Montrose, were the sons of the great lords and nobles of the country, who rubbed shoulders with those of the lesser gentry as well as with those of lower rank. They paid fees according to their families' fortune. The accounts of Montrose's tutor show that he had an enjoyable – if not particularly scholarly – time here, undertaking significant amounts of archery, golf, riding and other entertainment. He won the student archery competition in 1628, the prize for which was the duty to provide a silver medal to hang on the silver arrow – one of a remarkable set of seventy of these medals dating from the early seventeenth century until the mid-eighteenth, which are now on display in the University's museum.

Right: The signature of James Graham, earl (later marquis) of Montrose in the University's matriculation register. He signed on 26 January 1627, in company with his noble colleague, the earl of Sutherland.

[UYUY305/3]

Opposite: The archery medal won by the earl of Montrose in the student 'silver arrow' competition in 1628.

[Museum Collections, Archery Medal 8]

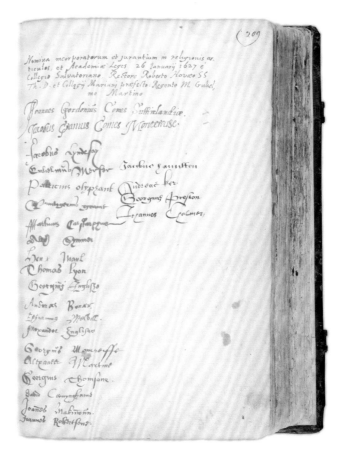

The picture we have of student life for the wealthy scholar in the seventeenth century is certainly less austere than Melville's diary paints for the more serious, religiously minded and relatively impoverished student of half a century earlier. Amongst those who signed the matriculation register with Montrose were the earl of Sutherland, a younger son of the earl of Moray, a son of the bishop of Orkney, and others who were the sons of gentry (although not all can be identified), described as *potens*, meaning that they were able to pay the highest level of fees. A few, like Montrose, went on to have careers in government, the military or high Church office, and live on in the history books. Most, however, were not so grand. There are far more who are described as *minus potens* – less wealthy, the sons of Church ministers, for example. One of them, Ephraim Melville, was the grandson of the diarist James Melville; like his father and namesake, Ephraim became a minister in the 'East Neuk' of Fife at Pittenweem, only a few miles from St Andrews.

Although none of Montrose's group are described in the records as *pauper*, there were no doubt also amongst them some who came from humbler homes. Of the twenty-four individuals whose subsequent careers are known, no fewer than eighteen of them went into the parish ministry, and it is noticeable that some of them had their careers cut short as a result of the religious and political turmoil which followed. At least one was the son of a merchant and, so far as we know, just two came from south of the border. One of the very striking features, however, is that of the twenty whose dates of death are known, only seven survived past the 1660s. Most of these men would have been born a year or two either side of 1610; half of them died before they reached their mid-fifties, and so far as we know only one of them reached the age of eighty.

One has the impression that St Andrews in the 1620s and 1630s was alive with activity; a place which then, as now, provided an environment where students from very different walks of life met, and where study and sociability went hand in hand. Certainly, there was a sense of optimism, if the physical development of the University is any guide. All of the colleges saw extensive building work in this period, not only in the interests of accommodating the increasing student numbers, but much of it also replacing or renovating property which had been on the verge of dereliction for many years, and erecting buildings which still remain integral to the University's 'historic core'.

The settled nature of the 1620s and 1630s, however, was not to last. James VI and I died in 1625 and was succeeded by his son, Charles I. Charles was less astute and subtle a ruler than his father had been, and it was not long before the sparks of controversy were once again kindled. At the heart of the dispute was not just the organisation of the Church, but also the way people worshipped. Like his father, Charles had a marked preference for episcopacy – bishops after all were royal appointees who might do the king's bidding – but he also favoured more elaborate and structured forms of worship, including kneeling at communion, which were alien to the Reformed Kirk in Scotland and perceived by presbyterian

To the left of archway, the seventeenth-century range of buildings on South Street which houses Parliament Hall and the King James Library. Started c.1612, it took upwards of thirty years to complete. The photograph was taken c.1845.

[Alb6-38]

divines as indistinguishable from Catholicism. James VI had also sought to reform the Scottish liturgy, bringing the Kirk more into line with the practices of the Church in England, but while James had been prepared to compromise, Charles was not. Within months of his accession to the throne he initiated a series of economic and constitutional changes that alienated the Scottish nobility, while also signalling his intention to impose a new prayer book, based on that in use in England, to which all of his Scottish subjects would be required to adhere. The result of these policies was to unite the Kirk and nobility in common opposition to royal policy.

The matter came to a head in 1637, when congregations in Edinburgh and elsewhere noisily and sometimes violently refused to allow their services to be conducted according to the new prayer book. Subsequently opposition to the king's religious reforms became organised, and in 1638 a committee known as the 'Tables' drew up a document famously known as the 'National Covenant', copies of which were circulated throughout the kingdom. The Covenant bound signatories in loyalty to the king – since this was not to be an act of rebellion – but it also bound them in opposition to any religious reforms which had not been approved by both the Kirk's General Assembly and by the Scottish parliament. A General Assembly of the Church, under the leadership of its moderator Alexander Henderson, the minister of Leuchars and a graduate of St Andrews (who had been an important member of the 'Tables' and was instrumental in drawing up the National Covenant), proceeded to annul most of the reforms introduced by both James VI and Charles I, including episcopacy itself. This was, of course, a massive challenge to royal authority in Scotland, and the first instinct of the University, probably because it feared an accusation of treason, was to remain true to the old order, and to refuse to adopt the National Covenant. Its opposition, however, did not last for long.

Charles I's response to the General Assembly's actions was, unsurprisingly, a military one. Although initially short-lived, further armed conflict was inevitable, and the reign of Charles I became increasingly tumultuous in both England and Scotland, as the king's attempts to impose his will in both political and religious terms created growing opposition. The result was that the 1640s saw outright rebellion and civil war in both countries, a confused situation in which religion and politics were inextricably tangled. The marquis of Montrose was a central figure, leading armies firstly in support of the Covenanting cause, and then, when he baulked at outright rebellion against the crown, in support of the king.

Eventually, in 1649, Charles I was condemned and executed by the English parliament, an action which horrified the Scots, who were absolutely unwilling to be party to regicide. They proclaimed the exiled son of the dead king to be Charles II, and attempted to get his agreement that they would support his monarchy in return for his acceptance of presbyterianism. He tried to avoid this by sending

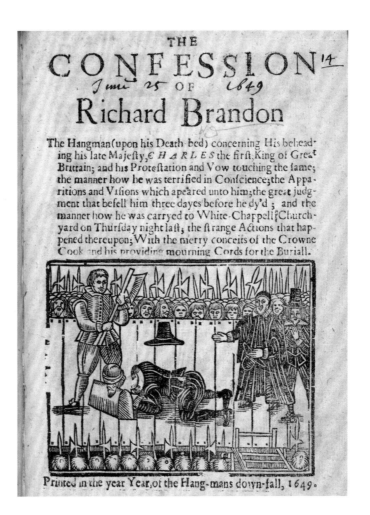

A graphic woodcut illustration of the execution of King Charles I: frontispiece to *The Confession of Richard Brandon the Hangman* (London, 1649).

Montrose with an army, but the force was defeated and Montrose himself was executed. Charles II came to terms with the Scots, and was crowned at Scone on 1 January 1651. England, however, was not prepared to accept Charles II as king. The English army, under the command of Oliver Cromwell, inflicted two heavy defeats on Scottish forces. The Scots armies destroyed, Charles had no option but once again to go into exile, and for almost a decade Scotland lost her independence, being part of Cromwell's 'Commonwealth', with English garrisons throughout the country.

The death of Cromwell saw Charles II restored to both crowns in 1660. However, religious tensions remained at a high pitch. Charles II insisted on the restoration of episcopacy and, while many Scots clergy conformed to the new settlement, others refused to do so, fomenting civil unrest that was often met with bloody persecution. Charles II died in 1685, to be succeeded by his Roman Catholic brother, James VII of Scotland and II of England, and the prospect of a future Catholic royal succession prompted increasing anxiety that culminated in the so-called 'Glorious Revolution' of 1688. This proved to be the permanent overthrow and exile of the main Stewart line. Despite a last-ditch military attempt in James' favour by an army led by John Graham, Viscount Dundee (another St Andrews graduate), James' son-in-law, William of Orange (the husband of James' daughter, Mary), was accepted both as King of England and as King of Scots.

It is clear that throughout these troubled times the corridors of power were walked by many with close connections to the University: Henderson, Montrose and Dundee, to name but a few. As a result of the religious persecution, many of the men who had gone into the parish ministry following their studies in the earlier part of the century lost their livings. As previously, however, the troubled nature of politics in the kingdom had a direct effect on the University itself, and the religious controversies which pervaded the period affected the scholarly community just as deeply as they did the rest of the nation.

The University's opposition to the Covenant did not last long, and the inevitable tide of reforming zeal once again swept through the institution. Two General Assemblies of the Kirk met in St Andrews, in 1641 and 1642, and, bolstered also by a decree from the parliament, a commission worked for several years once again to reform the University. Alexander Henderson was central to this work, and he was deeply concerned to make the University as effective as it could be for the pursuit of learning in the new era which the commissioners hoped to usher in. He personally gave the princely sum of £1,000 to enable completion of the building on South Street which had been started in the early years of the century to house a common hall and library; Parliament Hall and the King James Library were thus finally completed in 1643. The University's first librarian, John Govan, was appointed and funds were made available for the purchase of books. The constitution and organisation of the University and of the colleges were reviewed, resulting in clarification of the roles of the various officers and making significant amendments to the way in which, for instance, the Rector and

Chancellor were elected. For the first time the assembled senior academics of the University were constituted as a formal *Senatus Academicus* – the body which, to this day, makes academic policy and awards degrees. With an eye to the future training of the parish clergy, the commission also ordained that only the General Assembly of the Kirk had the right to appoint to the four posts of professor in St Mary's College; the Kirk was also to have some influence over other appointments throughout the University.

The curriculum was regulated (although it seems not to have altered fundamentally from earlier times), and a more modern system of teaching was introduced, finally replacing 'regenting' and dictation of notes with the professorial system and lectures. There was also an unsuccessful attempt to institute a common syllabus throughout all of Scotland's universities. As ever, the behaviour and lifestyle of the students and masters were subject to further scrutiny and regulation. Many of the reforms carried out by the commission in its early years were sound and thoughtful. As the political situation grew steadily more chaotic, however, the commission became increasingly concerned with the orthodoxy of the views of those within the University, and the religious intolerance which characterised the age was as prevalent in the University as elsewhere.

The modern interior of Parliament Hall.

The parliament which first indicted Montrose and his followers for treason in 1645/6 sat in the newly completed hall in South Street; as so often before, St Andrews was right at the centre.

The commission finished its work in 1649, and it seems that the decade of the Commonwealth was relatively peaceful, with the University able to continue its business relatively undisturbed. Men who were, or were to become, notable in their fields studied and taught here. Perhaps foremost among them was Samuel Rutherford, appointed the Professor of Divinity and Principal of St Mary's College by the General Assembly in 1639. Born about 1600, he had been educated in Edinburgh University, and had briefly been a regent there before entering the parish ministry for a while. A devoted presbyterian and Covenanter, Rutherford was a key figure in the complex and bitter politics of the period, and one whose religious belief informed and developed his political stance. He was the author of one of the most significant works of political theory of the age, *Lex Rex (The Law and the King)*, written as a justification for military resistance to Charles I. Drawing on political theory from across the ages, he expounded and developed the constitutional idea that there was a mutually beneficial contract between king and people which allowed the king to rule with the consent of the people. The king's breaking of the contract justified resistance to him. As Ronald Cant, a recent historian of the University, commented, 'there is still something dramatic in the thought that the most explosive political treatise of this whole period – the famous *Lex Rex* – issues from a St Andrews study'.

Rutherford was also one of the Scottish commissioners who attended the meetings between 1643 and 1649 which drew up, amongst other important

A seventeenth century oil portrait, thought to be of Samuel Rutherford, by an anonymous artist. It was donated to the University in 1908, but there is little information about its earlier history, which hinders investigation to prove or disprove the identity of either artist or subject.

[Museum Collections, HC223A]

documents, the Westminster Confession of Faith, which still informs the doctrine of many presbyterian churches throughout the world. Rutherford's unwavering opposition to any compromise on the issues of Church organisation and theology, and his well-known attitude to the limitation of royal power, did not endear him to the new regime after the restoration of Charles II in 1660; copies of his books were symbolically burned, he was deprived of his position in the University, and was even cited to attend trial for treason. Before the trial could take place, though, he died in St Andrews, in March 1661. His uncompromising attitudes must have made him difficult to work with, and we know that his time in St Andrews was not without dispute, either within the University or with the local religious authorities. Nonetheless, Rutherford must count amongst the University's luminaries.

Samuel Rutherford's *Lex Rex*, an 'explosive political treatise'. This copy has a title page which has been handwritten, probably in the eighteenth century, to replace the original, presumably missing.

[London, 1644;
r17 BX8915.R8L49C44B]

Some of his contemporaries left less controversial legacies. John Scot, for example, initially a student in St Leonard's College in the early years of the seventeenth century, pursued further study on the continent, leading to an eminent career at the Scottish bar. A Privy Councillor and a knight by his early thirties, his position of prominence exposed him to the ill effects of the religious and civil disturbances which blighted the country throughout his life. His greatest legacy, however, was as a man of letters. He endowed a Chair of Humanity in St Leonard's College, in 1620, and was a noted patron of the arts. A poet and author himself, he maintained regular contact with some of Europe's leading intellectuals from his estate of Scotstarvit, only a few miles from St Andrews. He sponsored publication by his friend Johannes Blaeu, the renowned Amsterdam printer, of what was the first anthology of Scottish poetry, *Delitiae Poetarum Scotorum* (1637), and was also responsible for the inclusion of Scottish maps within Blaeu's famous atlas. Having funded the revision of earlier maps drawn by Timothy Pont (another St Andrews alumnus), he involved himself intricately in their publication. He died in 1670, his life a proof that even in an age of turmoil and intolerance, the pursuit of learning was an inextinguishable flame.

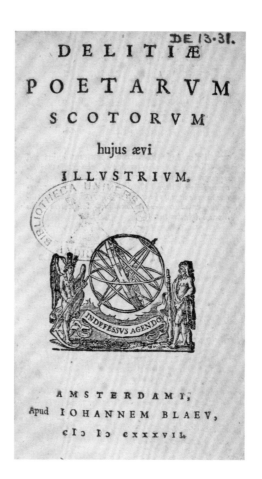

Delitiae Poetarum Scotorum, published by Blaeu of Amsterdam in 1637, with the financial support of John Scot of Scotstarvit.

[Typ NA.C37BJ]

Scotstarvit Tower, the home of
John Scot of Scotstarvit.

[Photograph by G. Alan Little;
GAL-231]

5

Adversity and endurance

The period following the restoration of the monarchy in 1660 was, as we have seen, another sad tale of conflict and warfare. In some respects St Andrews fared better than much of the country; being the ecclesiastical centre of the newly re-established episcopacy, the town and University saw a degree of investment, including substantial rebuilding of the St Salvator's College buildings. Even during the Commonwealth period, however, St Andrews was apparently less deprived than might have been expected. An agent of Cromwell's government, Thomas Tucker, who in 1655 visited Scotland to assess its potential for taxation, said that St Andrews 'hath formerly beene bigger, and although sufficiently humbled in the time of intestine troubles, continues still proud in the ruins of her former magnificence, and in being yett a seate for the Muses'.

James Sharp, an Aberdeen graduate who had been a regent in St Andrews in the 1640s, after a period in the parish ministry, was appointed Professor of Divinity in St Mary's College in succession to Rutherford early in 1661. Throughout the 1640s and 1650s he had espoused the Covenanting cause, and was another figure who was deeply engaged with the politics of the period. He had more readiness to compromise than Rutherford, though, and when episcopacy was restored under Charles II in 1661, he was ready to espouse it, and was appointed archbishop of St Andrews. A keen supporter of the University, he used his position to provide further endowment, particularly for St Mary's and St Leonard's Colleges. However, still inextricably involved on the national stage by virtue of his office, he was vilified by the increasingly intolerant remnants of the Covenanting movement, for whom allegations of corruption and dissolution added to a natural distaste for his position. He ended his life in 1679, the victim of murder at Magus Muir, only a few miles outside St Andrews. Opinions still differ regarding Sharp and his contribution to national life; he had been a friend to the University, however, and may thus have been at least partly responsible for the adherence by its senior figures to the principle of episcopacy, which was to be their downfall a decade later.

One indication of the favour in which the University was regarded in this period was the endowment of a professorship in Mathematics in 1668. This was a 'regius' chair – one endowed by the crown, and to which the crown had to approve appointees. The first Regius Professor of Mathematics must be amongst St Andrews' most successful academic appointments. Educated at Aberdeen

Opposite: The murder of Archbishop Sharp in 1679, as portrayed in the painting by John Opie RA (1797). The original hangs in the Museum of the University of St Andrews, and was purchased in 2007, with financial assistance from a private donor, The Art Fund, and the National Fund for Acquisitions.

[HC2008.9]

University, James Gregory subsequently spent time working and studying in London and on the continent, and produced several very well-received publications (including his most famous, *Optica Promota* (1663)) before being appointed to the chair in St Andrews. An influential figure in the development of both pure and applied mathematics, a contemporary, friend (and to some extent rival) of Isaac Newton, he has to be counted amongst the great scientific names of his day. A considerable amount of his scientific correspondence survives in the University Library's manuscript collections. Gregory's position in St Andrews, however, was difficult. His radical teaching techniques were viewed with suspicion by some of his colleagues, and the introduction of science into the curriculum was seen by some as a dilution of traditional educational values: academic conservatism was still alive and kicking, despite the reforming commission of the 1640s. He was tempted away to a Chair of Mathematics at Edinburgh University in 1674, but he died suddenly soon afterwards, still only in his late thirties. If his scientific legacy was far-reaching, so too was his personal one, since his purchase of equipment and espousal of new methods were to inform and encourage developments over succeeding generations of scholars.

Despite half a century of religious controversies, civil war and constitutional revolution, the University thus seemed to have prospered by the later seventeenth century. Some of the reforms so reluctantly accepted were apparently taking root, and by the 1680s the curriculum was developing, the college buildings and finances were in a better state than they had been a few decades earlier, and a

Optica Promota, James Gregory's renowned work on optics, which he published five years before he took up his chair in St Andrews.

[London, 1663; For QC383.G8O6]

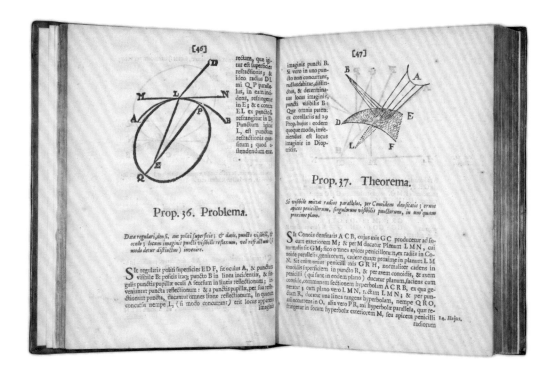

Right: James Gregory, Professor of Mathematics from 1668 to 1674. [GPS]

Below right: A Gregorian reflecting telescope, made by James Short of Edinburgh in 1736. This telescope is of the pattern invented by James Gregory. The original is on display in the Museum of the University of St Andrews.

[Museum Collections, PH206]

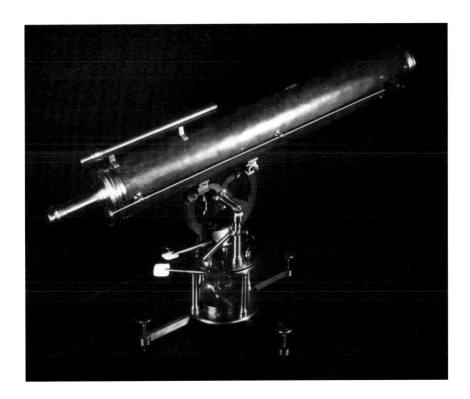

steady succession of influential alumni continued to make their mark on the world beyond St Andrews. Again, however, events outwith the University's control were to have a profound effect, highlighting a different side of the University's character in this period. When James VII and II eventually lost control and was forced into exile, the presbyterian-inclined government of William and Mary lost no time in once again abolishing episcopacy. The status of the seat of an archbishop was lost to St Andrews, and with it ecclesiastical pre-eminence, financial advantage, and the patronage of some of the most influential men in the realm. There was no immediate threat to the University, which retained its place as an important educational centre, but much of what gave the place its competitive edge was lost.

The immediate consequence of the political and religious revolution was inevitably another commission charged with reforming the Scottish universities. St Andrews, which had shown significant enthusiasm for the previous regime, had much to fear. The committee which began its work in St Andrews in August 1690 enquired thoroughly into the soundness of the doctrine and political allegiance held by the masters, their characters and lifestyles, and how assiduous they were in their duties, including not only their formal academic teaching, but also the extent to which they guided and mentored their students in matters of religious and moral conduct. It had all the hallmarks of inquisition. The proceedings of the commission survive in the National Archives of Scotland, and demonstrate that the University, under the leadership of its rector Dr Alexander Skene, was neither welcoming nor co-operative. When it came to the important business of swearing allegiance to the new king and queen, and accepting the new Confession of Faith, many of the masters simply did not turn up. They were awkward and uninformative in their evidence under questioning, and an attack on the integrity and character of the University as a whole by the civic author-ities – presenting a catalogue of sometimes violent injustice to the town and its people at the hands of uncontrolled students refusing allegiance to the new regime – provided a fatal blow.

The chairman of the visiting committee was the Earl of Crawford, himself Provost of St Andrews, who was no doubt happy to take the opportunity to redress the balance of power, which under normal circumstances placed the burgh authorities in subservience to the University. The town's indictment of the University, accusing the masters of failing to restrain the excesses of the students, and even of encouraging them, provides a picture of a tense and violent society within St Andrews. Weapons, ranging from mere snowballs to stones, swords, guns and clubs were commonly used by the students. The political and religious intolerance which increasingly characterised society had spilled over into the daily conduct of life, with evil consequence. The students were disruptive to Sunday worship, and appear to have terrorised the townsfolk; some of the masters were accused of drunkenness, and only a few were reckoned to have attempted to remedy the situation, with a complete lack of support from the senior members of the University. Whilst of course there may be an element of studied vindictiveness and political point-scoring in the onslaught which the University received, nonetheless it seems clear that the rule of the College statutes had broken down, and there was a degree of anarchy in the conduct of the University.

Unsurprisingly, the commission took a dim view of the vast majority of the evidence presented to it both from within and outwith the University. In the end, the commissioners reported that 'the Rector, principalls and regents of the universitie have been negligent in keeping good order in the said universitie and that some of them are guiltie of gross immoralities'. Their negligence and immorality, in combination with their contempt for the proceedings and their political and religious disaffection, led to most of the professors and senior masters of the University being deprived of their positions, to be replaced by men with more acceptable political and religious views. One of the excluded was James Gregory, Professor of Mathematics, nephew of his eminent predecessor, and the second of a dynasty of Gregories who were to hold chairs in the University for over a century. Over the next few years the commission continued its enquiries into the curriculum and teaching methods of all four universities (Edinburgh had by then joined St Andrews, Aberdeen and Glasgow, with a foundation in 1583), and in 1695 came up with a series of suggested reforms which were, with a few specific exceptions, largely uncontroversial. They did attempt once again to regulate the length of the academic year, and the style of examination, and suggested some alteration to the standard curriculum. It can have come as no shock that they also tried to correct the conduct of students and masters, dictating strictly their dress and behaviour.

It is curious, however, that three years before the commission reported, early in 1692, one John Row wrote to his uncle, who had asked him 'to give ane account of the Order and Discipline of this Colledge'. Whether the request had been made out of alarm at the news coming out from the commission's hearings, or just out of general familial interest, we do not know. What Row's four closely written pages describe, however, is a far cry from the drunken and violent excesses revealed to the commission. Row, who had been a student in St Leonard's College in the late 1670s (graduating in 1682), and was by 1691 a regent in the same college, went on to become a regent in Edinburgh University by 1695. What he describes is a sober life, lived primarily within the college walls, and regulated by the strict routine of prayers and devotions, classes and formal 'disputations', usually from awakening at 5.00 a.m. until bedtime at 9.00 p.m. He describes in detail the examination system, the teaching, the administrative structure of the University, and the system of discipline should any student misbehave. Each master, he tells us, rebukes or corrects their own scholars for 'private faults' such as negligence of their studies. 'Public faults' such as 'absence from publick prayers, speaking of English, swearing, curseing, playing at forbidden games, cartes, dyce etc., being the occasion of broil or tumults in the Colledge' were dealt with publicly by

St Andrews Aug. 10. 1691

Reverend Sir

My last was of the 11: of May, in Answer (at your desire) to Mr Rich: Strettons, to you, of the 19: of April. This by your direction, serves to give one account of the Order & Disciplin of this Colledge.

The Masters wear black gouns, the Students red; and all lodge w'tin the Colledge. The Colledge bell rings at 5: of the clock in the morning & immediatly there-after, in the winter-time, the Janitor goes to all the Students chambers, to Awaken any who are yet Asleep & to give light to any who take it: And both Sumer & winter A Regent (who for that week is called Hebdomader, which all the 5. are pr' vices) dos per, lustrat the Students chambers about 6: in the morning, to See that all be within the Colledge, & Studeously Employed: at 7: of the clock: the bell rings, & Masters & Students do all goe to publick prayers, where there is first read, by A fundation bursar (that is a poor Stu, dent maintained on the Colledge rents) A Chap: both in the old & new testament, & then the principal, if present, prays; in his absence the Hebdom: prays; there-after they Sing some verses of A psalm, & last of all the princip: or Hebd: pronunces the Blessing. presently after publick prayer, all the classes in the Colledge; which as pr my last are 5, goe to their respective privat Schools, & are taught by the Regents of the respective classes till 9: of the clock, at which time the bell rings for Break-fast: At 10: the classes are again conveened, by certan distinct ways of ringing the bell; The 3: philosophic classes, if they wryte any time for that day, do it betwixt 10 & 12: at which time the bell rings for Dinner: Upon Moonday Wedensday & fryday the Colledge gates are closs from 2. to 6. & on these 3: days the classes conveen (as in the fore-noon) & are taught by their own Regents till 6: at which time the bell rings, & all goe to publick prayers, as in the morning (every regent prays in his own school as-often as he can, w'een his Class, & dos order & take care that his scoolers perform their privat & secret Divotion in their chambers) After the publick prayer, in the Evening the bell rings for Supper; And again betwixt 8. & 9. (for at 9. the bell rings for goeing to Bed) the Hebdomad: dos again perlustrat all the Students chambers, as in the morning: On fenyday & Thursday in the after-noon the classes conveen not till 5. of the clock, & on Saturnday not at all in the After-noon; But on Saturnday morning, after publick prayers, All the Masters & Students in the Colledge conveen in the Comun scools, And 3. Students (being one in each of the 3. Superior classes) appointed by their own regent, do

Opposite: John Row's letter to his uncle in 1691, describing life in St Leonard's College.

[msLF1117.R6]

the college Principal and other masters 'according to the demerit of the crime'. Penalties might be fines, whipping ('in extraordinary cases, by all the masters') or exclusion.

Although his description relates specifically to life within St Leonard's College, Row presents us with the picture that we might expect of the University following the reforms proposed by the commission, not prior to them. Notably, he states that the regents daily went through the Confession of Faith with their classes, the negligence of which was a specific criticism by the commission. A student writing home might have reason to present a picture more sober than the reality: then, as now, there are some activities that it is better for parents and relatives not to know about. This was a regent, however, not a student. In an effort at self-preservation, there may have been an immediate disciplinary crackdown when the commission started meeting. Irrespective, Row's description of University life is detailed and believable enough to create a suspicion that the commission's damning indictment of every aspect of the University, and the appalling behaviour of staff and students alike, may have been exaggerated and was perhaps unjustifiably harsh.

The truth probably lies between the two pictures: hardly as bleak as had been painted in the interests of giving the commission an excuse to sweep clean, but not without conflict. The tensions between town and University erupted again in the late 1690s when a dispute between a University servant and a townsman ended in a grievous assault. There was a serious argument, lasting for two years, between the University and the civil authorities regarding the rights of jurisdiction in the case, and such was the ill-feeling over this matter that the University's Chancellor, John, Earl of Tullibardine, proposed that the University should be moved lock, stock and barrel to Perth. The second such proposal (James I had suggested it in 1426), it was not to be the last. Many of the University's staff appear to have welcomed it, and the scheme was seriously examined, to the extent of negotiating with the Perth authorities over the provision of suitable accommodation. The events of the 1690s had no doubt created a poisonous atmosphere between town and gown in St Andrews, which was in any case beginning to suffer in its post-archiepiscopal age.

Various reasons were produced in support of the 'transportation' of the University: St Andrews was unhealthy – 'now only a Village, where most part farmers dwell, the whole Streets are filled with Dunghills, which are exceedingly noisome and ready to infect the air, especially at this season when the herring guts are exposed in them'; the dissension between University and city made it 'impossible for us to keep Gentlemen and Noblemen's Children from incurring great hazards'; and the residents of the town were 'much sett upon tumuluating' and had an 'aversion and hatred . . . to Learning and Learned men'. This was apparently the University's opportunity to gain its revenge for the town's evidence against it to the commission at the beginning of the decade. Perhaps as a result of the tumultuous politics of the previous half century, it is likely that both

A View of the City of St Andrews taken from the North West

1   The Ruins of the Castle
2 2 2   The Ruins of the Cathedral
3   St Salvators Colledge
4   St Salvators Colledge Chapel
5   The Tolbooth
6   Trinity or Town Church

John Oliphant's depiction of
St Andrews in 1767, just a few
years before the visit of Johnson
and Boswell.

[Gra DA 890.S106, no.5]

stories tell us more about a failure in good town–gown relations than about the
true nature of either town or University. In the end, despite lengthy and detailed
negotiations with the authorities in Perth (who welcomed the proposal), no final
agreement was reached, the ongoing dispute over the assault in St Andrews was
settled, and the University remained where it had always been.

Within three quarters of a century, St Andrews had changed. Late in the
evening of Wednesday 18 August 1773 Dr Samuel Johnson, at the very start of
his *Journey to the Western Islands of Scotland* with James Boswell, drove into
the town after, according to his companion, 'a dreary drive, in a dusky night'.
An acute, if sometimes curmudgeonly, observer, Johnson was clearly excited at
the prospect of visiting the renowned town and University. He praised the ready
and cultured welcome and hospitality of his host, Robert Watson, Professor of
Logic, Rhetoric and Metaphysics. A St Andrews graduate and author of a well-
known history of King Philip II of Spain, Watson was closely acquainted with
some of the great men of the Scottish Enlightenment. When they viewed the
town the next day, however, Johnson was saddened by what he found, showing,
according to Boswell, 'strong indignation'. 'In the morning we rose to peramb-
ulate a city, which only history shews to have once flourished, and surveyed the
ruins of ancient magnificence, of which even the ruins cannot long be visible, unless

some care be taken to preserve them . . . They have been till very lately so much neglected, that every man carried away the stones who fancied that he wanted them . . . The city of St Andrews, when it lost its archiepiscopal pre-eminence, gradually decayed: One of its streets is now lost; and in those that remain, there is the silence and solitude of inactive indigence and a gloomy depopulation.' He complains of the sorry state of the University, in which he says there are only 100 students, and is critical of a society which, whilst increasing in economic prosperity, allowed its universities to decay. As they leave the city on the Friday, Johnson comments that 'whoever surveys the world must see many things that give him pain. The kindness of the professors did not contribute to abate the uneasy remembrance of an university declining, a college alienated, and a church profaned and hastening to the ground . . . Had the university been destroyed two centuries ago, we should not have regretted it; but to see it pining in decay and struggling for life, fills the mind with mournful images and ineffectual wishes.'

That the student population had apparently been more than halved in the course of a century; and that the town and university alike were clearly in a state of neglect and decay, demonstrates a reversal of fortunes which sits ill at ease with the importance with which the commission of the 1690s regarded the place of St Andrews within the educational life of the country. What had happened? Certainly it is true that with the loss of the episcopacy, St Andrews lost its pre-eminence as the centre of the country's religious life, depriving it of the patronage of some important people, and of revenue from the medieval ecclesiastical endowments, which had largely been confiscated to the secular authority. That, however, was not enough to account for the reverse. Again, the answer is less concerned with St Andrews itself than with national and international affairs.

Trade with the Americas was beginning to gain momentum by the end of the seventeenth century, and although Scotland's attempt at establishing its own trading colony at Darien in Central America in the 1690s had been a spectacular failure in both financial and human terms, the eventual political Union with England, which was controversially passed by both the Scottish and English parliaments in 1707, opened up trade with the English colonies to the eager Scottish merchants. Prior to this, the focus of Scottish sea trade had been as it was in medieval times: eastwards to Scandinavia and the Baltic. The east coast ports were the powerhouse of the Scottish overseas trading economy: reporting to Cromwell in the 1650s, Thomas Tucker had identified at least fifty trading vessels working out of the Fife ports. As part of the new United Kingdom, however, the focus of trade began to shift westwards, for the riches of the sugar, cotton, tobacco and slave trades of the colonies. This was the period in which Glasgow, for instance, began to develop, as merchants became rich through colonial trade. At the same time, of course, Union meant that the land routes to the south through England became easier. As a result the smaller-scale east coast trading activity declined, and with it the wealth and importance of east coast burghs, including St Andrews.

Above left: The village and harbour of Crail, c. 1880, one of the main centres of Fife's mercantile activity.

[Photograph by James Valentine & Co.; JV1461(B)]

Above right: St Andrews harbour, photographed by Robert Adamson and D.O. Hill in 1846. This was a thriving trading harbour in the 1650s when Thomas Tucker reported to Cromwell.

[Alb22-4]

Opposite: The journal of Alexander Gillespie, a trading skipper operating out of Elie on the Fife coast in the second half of the seventeenth century. Between 1662 and 1685 it details his activities at sea: the journeys he undertook, usually to Norway, the Baltic, Holland, and to Bordeaux for wine; his cargoes, the weather, and his adventures, including several brushes with pirates.

[ms38352]

Scotland was gradually moving away from the primarily agrarian economy which had characterised it for centuries. Since medieval times there had been a very gradual shift of population from rural, self-sufficient settlements to the growing burghs. Throughout the eighteenth century this trend accelerated, as farming methods became more efficient and used fewer people, and as the beginnings of industrial revolution concentrated the population in growing urban centres. But St Andrews, unlike nearby Dundee, failed to develop into such a centre. It is not clear why: East Fife had natural resources in its coal-fields, and it had a good commercial infrastructure. Perhaps St Andrews' harbour was inadequate, the policies of those who governed it were too conservative, or the transport network required more expenditure than local investors were prepared to commit. As urban development passed it by, combined with the loss of income from Church lands, it is clear that in financial terms alone both town and University were bound to struggle. Now, in addition, the University had also to compete with three other Scottish universities placed in much larger towns which, although they did not all face westwards, nonetheless had mercantile communities of a size and character that would benefit from the generally increasing prosperity of the age. St Andrews was at a clear disadvantage. As Johnson said in 1773, it was a sad indictment of Scotland 'that a nation, of which the commerce is hourly extending, and the wealth encreasing . . . and while its merchants or its nobles are raising palaces, suffers its universities to moulder into dust'. In this period all of the universities lacked an element of the formal governmental support which they had previously enjoyed, but St Andrews, without a significant urban population from which to draw its students, and without the solid base of endowment which the others enjoyed at least to some extent, was in a poor condition to compete.

The great political event of the early eighteenth century was undoubtedly the parliamentary Union with England. It did not, however, finally put paid to the political turmoil which had preceded it: the aftershocks of the political and religious troubles of the previous century took several decades to subside. The new regime was very aware of the fragility of its hold on power, particularly in some of the more remote (and particularly northern) areas of the country, where support for the Stewart line, and a tendency towards episcopalianism and Roman Catholicism lingered. The notorious 'massacre of Glencoe' in 1692, for instance, was less an act of clan aggression than a government attempt to coerce allegiance amongst its less amenable subjects. After the deaths of William and Mary, and subsequently of Queen Anne (Mary's younger sister) in 1714, all without direct heirs, the succession was settled on the house of Hanover, thus ending the direct Stewart line of monarchs. King George I was the son of the daughter of James VI's daughter Elizabeth. This succession was of course offensive to those who still lamented the ousting of James VII in 1689. He had died before the Union, in 1700, but his son, also James, kept the 'Jacobite' cause alive, known to his supporters as 'James VIII' and to his opponents as 'the Pretender'. There were several attempts to win back the throne for the Stewarts, the most significant being in 1715 and 1745, when Jacobite risings once again raised the spectre of serious armed conflict. Both ended in defeat, the '45 on the bleak field of Culloden, near Inverness, where the Jacobite army was brutally destroyed by a government force led by the Duke of Cumberland in April 1746, the last pitched battle on British soil. Both rebellions, however, had caused serious discomfort to the government.

A diagram of the battle of Culloden, published in the Edinburgh newspaper the *Caledonian Mercury* on Thursday 1 May 1746.

[per AN3.C2]

As had been the case throughout its history, St Andrews was neither insensible to, nor unaffected by, the political events of the day. The purge which followed the Revolution of 1689 was the action of an insecure new regime; the Jacobite rebellions led to similar insecurity in the new Hanoverian monarchy. Given the traditionally pro-episcopalian stance of the University, it is hardly surprising that its loyalties were at best mixed when once again challenged by political upheaval. Certainly, there had been a change of personnel at the top which one might suppose would create in the institution an enthusiasm for the new order, but the University was more than just its leaders and, as it had demonstrated several times before, it would take more than the actions of one commission to alter fundamentally the traditions and culture of the institution. Suspicions of Jacobite leanings in the University were not ill-founded, and although there is no discernible 'official' policy of support for the cause, there is plenty of evidence to suggest that on a personal level there was a fair amount of Jacobite sympathy. In 1715/16 there was considerable Jacobite military activity in the area; in September 1715 the St Andrews authorities raised the local militia for defence of the town, and whilst there is no mention of it having been engaged in action, for some months there were Jacobite forces nearby, a fact which clearly encouraged some of their supporters openly to demonstrate their enthusiasm for the cause.

There were numerous complaints against individuals for drinking the health of the Pretender or similar seditious acts: in February 1716 one unfortunate (if belligerent) student of St Leonard's College, Arthur Ross, after a complaint from the civil authorities, was condemned by the Rectorial court to be whipped by his regent, fined, stripped of his gown and 'extruded' from the University. Similarly, action was requested by the town magistrates against a group of students who had

The minute of the University Senatus recording the expulsion of Arthur Ross from the University for his Jacobite activities.

[UYUY452/2 p.266]

rung the St Leonard's College bells in celebration of the news that the uprising had started. A considerable number of the leading Jacobite sympathisers, including those who, like Simon Fraser of Lovat, played very active roles in one or both of the rebellions, had close ties to St Andrews, having been students there, or having other connections (such as, in one case, being the son of the University's Chancellor). Some staff also had openly Jacobite leanings, and would do little to curb the exuberant rebelliousness of the youngsters. Naturally, this behaviour did not endear the University to the government.

Another commission visited the University in 1718, and although they were much less draconian than the previous visitors, at least one academic (Alexander Scrymgeour, Professor of Ecclesiastical History) lost his chair. There were good effects arising from the visitation: it was critical of the dilapidated condition of some of the college buildings, for instance, and instituted building programmes to renew them; and indeed its main efforts went into the overhaul of financial and administrative procedures, rather than personal vendettas against members of staff. Part of the rebuilding had been necessitated by a serious fire in St Leonard's College in 1702, the damage from which had not been repaired. Fire was always a threat, and in 1727 it destroyed a substantial part of St Mary's College and claimed the life of Scrymgeour's successor to the Chair of Ecclesiastical History, James Haldane. The University's contribution to the rebuilding of the College on this occasion was merely to allow it to use one year of the salary released by the deceased professor!

In the aftermath of the 1745 rebellion a serious witch-hunt was instituted against any who had taken part in, or been sympathetic to, the uprising. This resulted in further religious persecution and in the forfeiture of the lands of many of the eminent landowners and noblemen, particularly of the north; it was ultimately responsible for much of the social and economic change which led to radical alteration of highland society, emigration and depopulation of broad swathes of the country. It also removed from political and economic influence an entire generation or more of those who would traditionally send their sons to be educated in St Andrews. This, in combination with the other religious, social and economic factors, alongside a reluctance on the part of those who were firm in their allegiance to the new monarchy to patronise an institution which had a reputation for sedition, meant that a continuing decrease in student numbers was inevitable. As the numbers dropped, the financial position worsened and the town declined, so the reputation of both town and university suffered in a spiral of decay. The University had learnt the lesson of its earlier mistakes, however. At the end of the 1745–6 Jacobite rebellion, in the aftermath of Culloden, irrespective of the sympathies of some of the masters and students, the University made a spectacular demonstration of loyalty by offering the vacant University chancellorship to the duke of Cumberland, son of King George II and leader of the victorious government army. He accepted, and remained Chancellor for almost twenty years. There is not a great deal of evidence that he was either particularly enthralled with his official position or that he used his royal influence to benefit the University. At least, however, this time there was no political or religious inquisition or purge.

It would be wrong, however, to portray the eighteenth century as a period of unmitigated disaster for the University. Inevitably, declining fortunes led to some difficulty in maintaining the quality of professorial staff: reputation and resource have always been key factors in attracting and retaining the best people. There were beacons in the darkness, however. Thomas Simson was an excellent appointment (in 1722) to a new Chair in Medicine and Anatomy, the endowment of which by the duke of Chandos, who later became Chancellor, was one notable success of the period. Despite perhaps bolstering the Jacobite reputation of the University by being the son-in law of a rebel who had been forfeited for his part in the 1715 uprising, Simson was a good teacher (flouting the norms of the period by teaching in English), and held the chair until his death in 1764, when he was succeeded in it by his own son. His collection of books still graces the shelves of the University Library.

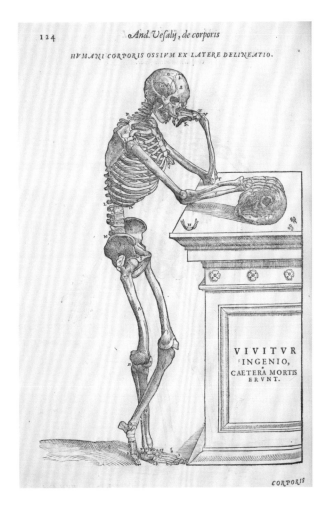

A plate from a sixteenth-century anatomical text, Andrew Vesalius, *De Humani Corporis Fabrica* (Venice, 1668), from the library of Thomas Simson

[Sim QM21.V2]

Despite the new chair, medical teaching at St Andrews was quite minimal until much later. There was a great deal of competition from the established medical schools elsewhere in the country, and the cost of setting one up in St Andrews would have been prohibitive. The University had previously awarded occasional medical degrees: the first known was to John Arbuthnot, who gained his MD on the basis of a successfully defended thesis in 1696. From around the turn of the eighteenth century, however, the practice became more common of awarding medical degrees *in absentia* upon submission of both an appropriate fee and personal testimonials by eminent physicians affirming the candidates to be both qualified and experienced. The number of such degrees rose steadily, and the practice became quite lucrative. From a modern standpoint it is easy to criticise this apparent abuse of degree-awarding powers. However, it should be remembered that the standard route into medicine in those days was through a general education followed by practical experience as a surgeon. The insistence on testimonial rather than a systematic medical education was therefore not out of step with the norm, and this was a trade in which St Andrews was by no means unique. Many celebrated doctors received their MD degrees from St Andrews, including Jean Paul Marat, luminary of the French Revolution, William Beattie, the surgeon who tended Nelson on board HMS Victory at the Battle of Trafalgar, and Edward Jenner, who gained fame through his pioneering work on vaccination against smallpox. Eventually, examination was demanded before the degree could be awarded, but a complete medical course was not taught by the University until the institution of the Conjoint Medical School with University College, Dundee, in 1898.

Two very different depictions of Jean Paul Marat: the fiery revolutionary, and the thoughtful intellectual. He was awarded a medical degree by the University of St Andrews in 1775.

[GPS]

Amongst other successes in the latter part of the century have to be counted the professorships of Robert Watson, who so nobly entertained Johnson and Boswell, William Wilkie in Natural Philosophy, and David Gregory, another of the startling clan of Gregories who so ably monopolised the Chair of Mathematics for almost the entire century. Students of the period were certainly fewer in number, and fewer still actually graduated: a symptom of the decline was that the examination system leading to the award of degrees partially broke down, and many students who undertook their full courses of study contented themselves with the learning they received from their masters, without undergoing the expensive ritual of graduation. Nonetheless, the University was not without its successful students. For example, Adam Ferguson, one of the great philosophers of the Scottish Enlightenment graduated from St Andrews in 1742. Amongst those who did not complete degree courses in this period, however, were figures of the eminence of James Wilson (1757/8–1760/1), one of the authors of the US constitution, who came from Carskerdo, a farm close to the nearby town of Ceres; and Robert Fergusson (1764/5–1767/8), the poet whom Robert Burns considered 'by far my elder brother in the Muse'. Burns himself attended no University, but St Andrews has the distinction of having educated the Scottish poet whom he regarded above all others.

Even if the situation was not completely hopeless, it cannot be denied that the University sadly declined through much of the eighteenth century; falling student numbers represented a problem which could have been terminal, had no action been taken to make the institution more viable. It was largely due to the foresight and tenacity of Thomas Tullideph, the Principal of St Leonard's

Below left: An oil portrait of Adam Ferguson, who graduated from St Andrews in 1742, by J. T. Nairn. Painted in 1813, it shows the renowned philosopher at the age of 90.

[Museum Collections, HC167]

Below right: James Wilson, one of the fathers of the American constitution, who studied at St Andrews from 1757/8 to 1760/1.

[GPS]

College, that the situation was rescued in the face of predictable opposition from the more conservative elements within the University. It was becoming clear that the declining University could not survive without radical surgery to reorganise and revive it. A proposal was made in 1737 to unite the three colleges into one, thus achieving economies of scale in terms not only of property, but also of salaries and other costs: to support three colleges with a student population which had previously filled one, was not feasible. Tullideph, taking up the principalship in 1738 (having previously been Professor of Divinity in St Mary's College), strenuously worked for the union and, after some years of negotiation, achieved partial success. St Mary's College did not participate, but agreement was eventually reached to amalgamate the two remaining colleges into 'The United College of St Salvator and St Leonard in the University of St Andrews', a scheme which was approved by parliament in June 1747. It was a bold and controversial move, overturning more than two centuries of tradition and history, but it was probably the salvation of the University.

The new College was housed on one site, that of St Salvator which, although in poorer repair than St Leonards, was the larger of the two, and had more space for potential expansion. Building work which was necessary to bring it to an acceptable standard continued for many years. The buildings of St Leonard's

The commonplace book of Thomas Tullideph, Principal of St Leonard's College at the union of the colleges in 1747.

[msLF1109.T8C6]

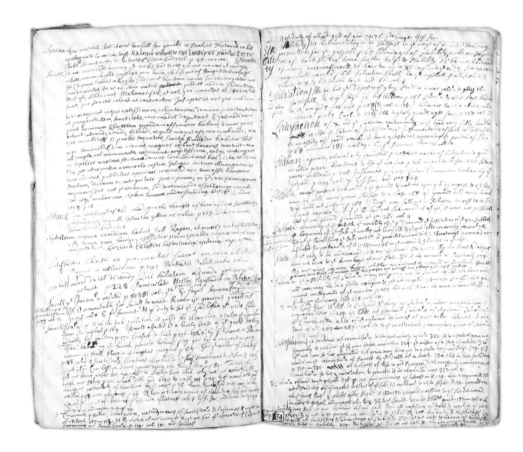

were effectively abandoned for University use: the college accommodation was first rented out and then sold (to Professor Watson, who entertained Johnson and Boswell in it); and the medieval chapel became derelict until eventually the University renovated it in the twentieth century. Its function as a parish church was moved first to the 'town church', Holy Trinity, and then in 1761 to St Salvator's chapel, where it remained until the opening of the new St Leonard's Parish Church in 1904, leaving St Salvator's chapel for University use.

The amalgamation of the fabric of the colleges was a practical matter. To create one academic community out of two, however, was potentially a much more emotional and complex task. Two professorships were vacant at the time of union, and several subsequent retirements left a body consisting of the Principal (Tullideph) and seven professors, five of whom had transferred from the old colleges. The two other chairs, of Mathematics and Medicine, had been endowed originally not within a college, but within the University as a whole. The professorial establishment of the College was thus to be a Principal, a Professor of Logic, Rhetoric and Metaphysics, a Professor of Ethics and Pneumatics, a Professor of Natural and Experimental Philosophy, a Professor of Greek, a Professor of Civil History, a Professor of Humanity, a Professor of Mathematics, and a Professor of Medicine. It was a far cry from the old system of regenting, where the same master taught a body of students all of their subjects throughout their degree. That particular reform, encouraged but only partially effected by Melville a century and a half earlier, had been long and slow in coming, but the union of the colleges finally made it permanent.

The teaching establishment also demonstrates how the old medieval curriculum had been changed. Robert Crawford and others have argued that St Andrews was one of the first universities to teach English literature, partly because some within Scotland in the immediate post-Union period had an aspiration to rectify 'barbarous' language and manners to help with assimilation into the more prosperous southern society. The original intention of the duke of Chandos (an English nobleman) had been to found a chair not of medicine, but of 'Eloquence', but the University had persuaded him that medicine was a more immediate concern. Nonetheless, in the context of his rhetoric classes, Professor Watson was one of the first professors in the world to teach English literary criticism. It was not uncontroversial: the Scots vernacular poet Robert Fergusson, who had been one of Watson's students, satirically lambasted the notion that social advancement was to be gained through the anglicisation of Scottish culture. In his poem 'To the Principal and Professors of the University of St Andrew's, on their superb treat to Dr. Samuel Johnson' Fergusson noted:

> . . . never send
> For daintiths to regale a friend,
> Or, like a torch at baith ends burning,
> Your house'll soon grow mirk and mourning.

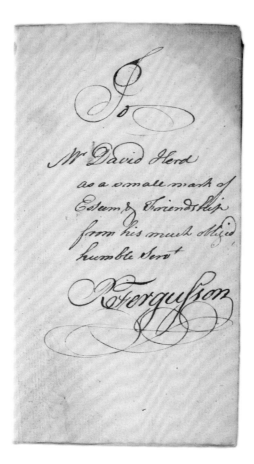

Above left: A copy of the *Poems* of Robert Fergusson (Edinburgh, 1773), inscribed in his own hand as a gift to his friend, David Herd.

[Typ BE.D73BF]

Above right: Robert Fergusson was not popular with all of his contemporaries in St Andrews. Anonymous student graffiti in this copy of Swift's *Miscellanies* (London, 1727, vol. 4), is thoroughly abusive of him.

[s PR3724.M4D27]

Mathematics and medicine were by now well established in the curriculum, despite the antagonism when the Chair of Mathematics had been established in 1668, and science was further represented by 'Natural and Experimental Philosophy', which we would now recognise as the precursor of modern physics, and for which there was a proposal to establish a course in 1714. Civil History was also a new discipline, in accordance with the eighteenth-century development of historiographical thought and technique; although it was not, in reality, effectively or regularly taught in St Andrews for several generations to come.

In the latter part of the eighteenth century great thinkers of the Scottish Enlightenment such as David Hume and Adam Smith were leading Scotland to the forefront of European intellectual activity. The universities of Edinburgh and Glasgow were certainly at the centre of this activity but, with a few exceptions, St Andrews in this period was not in the same league. Too many years of decline had taken their toll, and Johnson's lament for past magnificence and his indignation at the neglect were quite justifiable. He also lamented the union of the colleges as a symbol of the decay. In that, however, he was wrong, for it is quite probable that the union of the colleges saved the University from obliteration, and set it on a course which enabled it to take advantage of the new opportunities of the coming age. Thirty-five years had passed between the union of colleges and the visit of Johnson and Boswell, and by the end of the century the University was extant, but still basically a small provincial college in a rural setting.

When George Dempster (a well-known agriculturalist, and member of a family with long St Andrews connections) wrote in 1801 to a friend recommending his old *alma mater* for the education of his sons, he stated that he could offer 'nothing but encomiums' regarding the place. But his enthusiasm lay in the very aspects of the place which presented it with such difficulties. 'A young man can get no harm there. It is a healthy retired spot . . . A boy must learn there virtuous and economical habits.' And whilst Dempster praised the 'perfect' teaching of the University, he was clear that the students should be attended by a private tutor in addition to their formal courses. It was, even in those days, a limited and old-fashioned picture which he painted.

The letter of George Dempster to his friend in 1801, recommending St Andrews as a safe and wholesome place for a young man to undertake his education.

[ms38422]

At the dawn of the nineteenth century the Principal of St Mary's College was George Hill, who had been Professor of Greek in the United College since 1772. A distinguished theologian, in 1788 he was appointed Professor of Divinity in St Mary's College, and became its Principal from 1791 until 1819. Hill's principalship was marked by excellent scholarship both on his own part and that of others within the University. It was also characterised by raging controversy. A significant issue was that of nepotism. Hill himself was the nephew of the Principal of United College between 1781 and 1799, Joseph McCormick, and there seems little doubt that his promotion owed not a little to the relationship. In turn, Hill himself favoured his relatives, and for a time almost half of the University's Senatus were related to each other.

A predictable result of this system of 'patronage' was that the University was riven by personal dispute and dynastic jealousy. A letter dated 7 December 1810 from Robert Haldane, Professor of Mathematics in United College (and later to be Hill's successor as Principal of St Mary's), requests the opinion of the Chancellor of the University, Henry Dundas, 1st Viscount Melville, regarding the appointment to the Chandos Chair of Medicine. According to Haldane, the current professor, James Flint, wished to resign on account of his age and poor health, and had requested that the chair be given instead to his son, John. Wishing 'to gratify a worthy old man for whom I entertain the most sincere respect', Haldane was in one way keen to accede to James Flint's wish. On the other hand he had some concerns: 'In the first place I am a perfect stranger to the man for whom my vote is solicited. I never saw him, and never heard any thing particular about his Talents and Professional merit.' In addition, he refers to recent 'feuds and factions' which have 'distracted' and 'impaired' the University, and notes that Flint younger would be 'a Gentleman who from recent circumstances must be the most obnoxious man in the whole kingdom to the opposite Party'. Indeed, there had been an attempt in 1804 to have John associated in the chair alongside his father, but although the election was not quashed by the Senatus until 1809, the serious ongoing dissension amongst parties within the University over the issue had resulted in it being decided eventually by a judgement of the House of Lords. Haldane, clearly a supporter of Hill, notes that if Hill's opponents within the University 'had it within their power, they would nominate the most hostile man they could find to Dr Hill'. Haldane goes on to describe the ideal criteria for filling the post which, remarkably to modern minds, includes only brief reference to medical knowledge: 'He should be a respectable Physician.' The other criteria are soundness of principles in 'church and state', and his competence to teach chemistry, an ability which the University currently lacked. Tangentially, Haldane makes it clear that the appointee, whoever it should be, should also be of service 'in strengthening Dr Hill's party & . . . banishing bad blood from the University'.

Hill's 'party' was largely dynastic. His brother Henry succeeded him in the United College Chair of Greek in 1789; George's half-brother John was

Above left: Oil portrait of George Hill, Principal of St Mary's College from 1791 to 1819, attributed to John Watson Gordon.

[Museum Collections, HC189]

Above right: Robert Haldane, Professor of Mathematics, and then Principal of St Mary's College. This is a very early photograph, taken c.1845, either by Dr John Adamson or by his brother, Robert Adamson and D.O. Hill.

[Alb6-37-2]

Professor of Humanity from 1773 until 1775 (when he resigned to take up a chair in Edinburgh University, where his maternal grandfather, John Gowdie, had been Principal from 1754 to 1762); John Cook, who in 1802 was appointed to the Chair of Hebrew in 1802, and to the Chair of Biblical Criticism in 1808, was George Hill's brother-in-law; Cook's father, also John, was Professor of Humanity and then of Moral Philosophy between 1769 and 1815; in the third generation, another John was to be Professor of Ecclesiastical History from 1860 to 1868, and his brother George became Professor of Moral Philosophy in 1828. The picture develops of a very extensive network of family relationships, in which dynastic considerations outweigh any others. The Cooks and Hills were extensive and prolific local families, and despite the undoubted academic talent which they displayed, the influence they and their relatives exerted over the University for a period of almost a century has been described as a 'dead hand'. In this atmosphere, the politics of dynasty and feud tended to promote a slavish adherence to tradition, inhibiting the influx of new blood and stifling creativity.

To judge these patterns of behaviour by modern standards would be misguided, however. The career of the Chancellor to whom Haldane wrote in 1810 exemplifies the situation. Educated at Edinburgh University, Henry Dundas was called to the Scottish bar in 1763. He was at the height of his career and a figure central to Edinburgh society during the peak of the Scottish Enlightenment, when intellectual endeavour seemed to spring from the very cobblestones of the city. By 1775 he was Lord Advocate for Scotland, a position which wielded enormous power, being in effect the London government's 'manager' of Scotland. In ensuing years Dundas achieved extraordinary control over Scottish affairs; he largely managed the electoral system, thus effectively nullifying political opposition, and established a complex and efficient system of patronage which he used to control appointments to a wide range of public positions, including some university chairs.

George Hill and Henry Dundas were friends and close allies. When elected to the position of moderator of the General Assembly of the Church of Scotland in 1789, Hill had already been a prominent figure in Church politics for almost a decade. He managed the affairs of the Church in the Dundas interest, and as a result gained powers of patronage himself. Henry Dundas' Chancellorship lasted from 1788 until 1811. Although his influence waned somewhat in the last few years, in Dundas St Andrews University had gained a Chancellor with unrivalled political power, and his alliance with George Hill had been greatly in the University's interest. That Hill's half-brother gained a chair in Edinburgh University, and that one of Hill's sons became Professor of Divinity in Glasgow, demonstrate that the patronage system exercised at St Andrews in this period was not unique but was consistent with a more general feature of society.

Notwithstanding its privileged position, the picture we have of life within the University in this period, especially in its upper echelons, is not an attractive one. Nepotism inevitably led to self-interest and the factionalism which has already been described, and this rippled out to the disadvantage of others. During the latter years of the eighteenth century, for example, the custom of students living in college almost disappeared. The Hill regime discouraged it, partly because it was a burden to the college finances: if students lived elsewhere, the professors' salaries could be increased. In addition, the students forced to seek accommodation elsewhere frequently found it in the homes of the professors or their extended families, to whom they paid considerable rent. Doubtless the accommodation was more salubrious than it had been in the ageing college buildings, but the net effect was a clear influx of cash into the pockets of the professors, whose workload was at the same time reduced by the loss of college supervisory duties.

Since the purging commission of the 1690s, the University had suffered immense difficulties, and for much of the eighteenth century it was a shadow of its former self. While enlightened intellectual achievement in other parts of Scotland flourished, St Andrews seemed out on a limb, torn apart by factionalism and in decline. The picture is not completely bleak, however: there was academic success to celebrate, and the unification of the colleges did much to render the institution financially sustainable. The University had endured through adversity, and could look forward to a more secure future.

A caricature by John Kay of
Henry Dundas, Viscount Melville,
'manager' of Scotland and friend
of George Hill, Principal of St
Mary's College. From *A Series of
Original Portraits and Caricature
Etchings by the Late John Kay*

[Edinburgh, 1842]

6

Beyond recognition

On 16 February 1797 sixteen-year-old Alexander Berry and his slightly younger friend, George Walker, signed their names on the matriculation register of the University. They had been best friends at school in the nearby town of Cupar, and had no doubt travelled to St Andrews together at the start of session in the previous October for their next great adventure; they paid their first visit to the University Library together – in itself perhaps quite an adventure, if one believes Berry's later statement that they and their other friends were 'at constant feud with the crusty, ill-tempered old Librarian'! One can picture the two companions' excitement as they explored their new world. Their subsequent careers could hardly have been more different, however. Walker completed his degree and further studies, and took the traditional route of a career in the parish ministry, becoming the minister of Kinnell near Forfar, where he served with distinction for almost fifty-five years, and gained a reputation as a fine classical scholar. Berry, on the other hand, left St Andrews after only two years, and moved to Edinburgh, where he studied medicine. In 1801 he received the diploma of the Royal College of Surgeons. He had intended to go into the Royal Navy, but his father dissuaded him and he set off instead as a ship's surgeon with the East India Company, heading for China.

Walker and Berry lost touch, but in 1867, on the other side of the world, Berry read in a newspaper that Walker had been awarded an honorary degree by the University of Edinburgh; it reminded him of their friendship, and a correspondence between them ensued. Before Walker's death just a year later they were able to exchange only a few letters at such distance. Berry's letters, however, which are preserved in the University library, are long and full of the detail of his amazing life. It was a career of extraordinary adventure, including several shipwrecks, a few brushes with cannibals and pirates, an attack of yellow fever, political intrigue and ocean-going travels in every part of the globe. He had soon given up his medical career. Opting instead for the merchant life, he eventually settled in Australia, and became the massively wealthy owner of an estate in New South Wales. Late in life he recalled that, having been born on a wild, tempestuous night, it had been 'perhaps an indication of a stormy life'. His birth-night, however, was St Andrew's Day, and 'St Andrew never seems to have left my side; I have passed through many dangers and have weathered many a storm and, thank God, never yielded to despair'. Cutting short his degree studies

The signatures of Alexander Berry and George Walker in the University's Matriculation Register. Berry's signature is immediately above that of another close childhood friend, Alexander Nimmo.

[UYUY309]

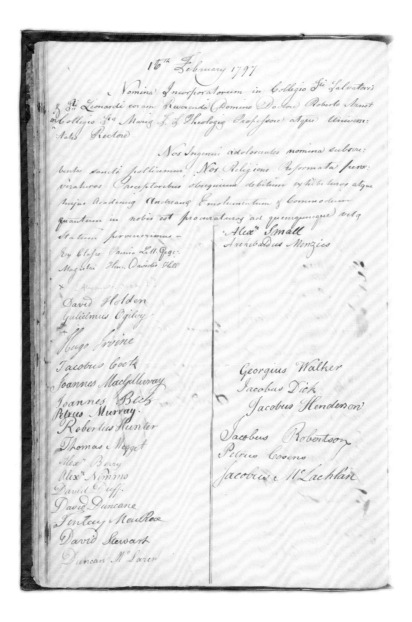

in St Andrews was no indication of a lack of intellect. Merchant and adventurer, he was also a founder member of the 'Philosophical Society of Australia'. He published a well-regarded scientific paper on the geology of the coastline near his estate, and collected minerals and anthropological specimens, which he gave to what is now the Royal Museum of Scotland in Edinburgh. He also became involved in politics, as a member of the New South Wales legislature. The letters don't tell much about the young friends' student days, but, in response to Walker's sending him a copy of the University of St Andrews *Calendar*, he comments that he is 'most delighted with the resuscitation of St Andrews'.

It is not from the letters that we learn that the pair visited the library together. That information comes from the library's own records which, for a period of almost two centuries, preserve in leather-bound volumes the lists of books borrowed by the students and their professors. They are a rich source of information about studying habits and the development of subjects, and enable us to see the way in which, from the faltering early beginnings, the library had become a focal point of everyday student life. The earliest reasonably complete library catalogue still in existence lists roughly 1,600 printed books and manuscripts which the University owned by 1695. A century later, the library used by Berry and Walker had grown enormously, partly because of some generous benefactions and gifts, but more especially because in 1709 the Copyright Act gave St Andrews, like the other university libraries, the right to claim copies of every new book published in the British Isles. The right was not always exercised, but it does mean that the library's collections of books published between 1710 and 1836 (when the privilege was withdrawn in return for a modest annual cash payment)

were, and still are, outstanding. After 1836 the pace of growth seems not to have slowed: the trend had been set, and by purchase, gift and bequest, the library continued to grow throughout the nineteenth century. In 1864 the catalogue which had occupied only 43 handwritten pages in 1695, required no fewer than 45 volumes, each of 200 pages. A rough calculation suggests that the population of the library at the end of the century would have been in the region of 150,000 titles. The library building, of course, was adequate for the support neither of such a collection nor of an increasing student body, and so the seventeenth-century building on South Street was twice extended and remodelled, in 1889–90 and 1907–9.

The growth in the library is symptomatic of a change in the University which went far beyond just its size; from the early days, when only Aristotle was good enough, the curriculum had expanded. Walker existed on a diet overwhelmingly of history and classics, supplemented by a few other works which almost certainly were recommended to him – or perhaps forced on him – by the ever-enthusiastic Berry. Berry's own reading, however, went far beyond the requirements of his studies (and, one suspects, largely ignored much of the course!). He read especially about travels, exploration, and natural history. Glancing down the list, we have *Cook's Voyages*, a *Collection of Voyages*, *Hawksworth's Voyages*, Buffon's *Natural History*, Vailant's *Travels*, *Voyage to California*, Smellie's *Philosophy of Natural History*, Thalm's *Travels*, Gray's *Tour in Germany*, and Marsden's *History of Sumatra*. Many of the books he read are still in the library today. Students in this

The late nineteenth-century extension to the South Street library.

period were expected to read widely, and they bought some of their own books: the detailed personal accounts kept in the 1820s by another student, Duncan Dewar, shows him purchasing works by Homer, Aeschylus, Livy, Ovid, Horace, Euripides, Virgil and Bunyan, as well as Latin, Greek and Scots dictionaries, and other works on Philosophy, Logic, Rhetoric, French, Mathematics, Anatomy, History, Scots, English and European Literature, Theology, Church History and other subjects. In addition, his library borrowing record shows him reading Plutarch, Buchanan and Rousseau, as well as a wide range of modern historical, literary and other texts.

Berry died, at the respectable age of ninety-one, in September 1873, a world apart, almost literally, from his birthplace on the farm outside Cupar. He seems

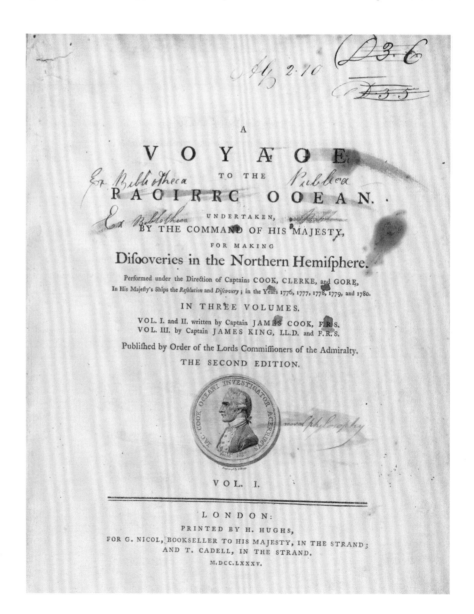

James Cook's *A Voyage to the Pacific Ocean ...*, vol. 1 (London, 1775): the very copy borrowed by Alexander Berry in 1797.

to have retained an affection for the University, and in accordance with his wishes his brother later gave a handsome gift which was used, amongst other things, to endow a Chair of English Literature, the Berry Chair, which still exists. Walker's legacy to the University was no less; a charitable trust was established in his memory by his younger brother for the purpose of 'furthering the usefulness or relieving the needs of the University of St Andrews', which still supports worthy academic causes within the University.

The stories of Berry and Walker serve to illustrate how much the world had changed for a student entering, and more particularly leaving, the University. Berry commented on this: 'What a change a hundred years have made, a voyage round the world is now an everyday occurrence . . . We have lived in eventful times[:] about the period of our birth, the British American Colonies had obtained their independence, but which eventually occasioned the colonisation of the Australian colonies. A hundred years ago New South Wales was a terra incognita.' If the world had in one sense grown through exploration, then it had also become far smaller through navigational advances and the improvements in the technology of transport. Berry and Walker doubtless walked between Cupar and St Andrews; only twenty-five years later, Duncan Dewar walked twenty-five miles from his home beside Loch Tay to Perth, from where he took a steamer to Dundee and a ferry to the south side of the River Tay.

The changes in society went deeper than that, however, amounting to a revolution which had far-reaching effects across every level of British society. Advances in agricultural methods allowed more intensive production using fewer people. Migration from rural areas to towns and cities, already considerable in the eighteenth century, thus accelerated enormously in the early nineteenth century, especially in the central belt. As the 'clearances' of highland estates took place in waves throughout much of the nineteenth century, in what was at times a shocking social and economic 'experiment', the mass migration both to urban centres within Britain and to far-flung lands resulted in a marked alteration of Scotland's demographic patterns. The economy thrived as new technologies enabled greater production of exportable goods, and improvements to transport – road, rail and canal building – eased and speeded the movement of people and raw materials. The industrial age was further stimulated by expanding colonial markets and by a constant demand for goods and materials to supply the military machine which fought apparently endless wars in many parts of the world.

Naturally, social, demographic and economic change caused social and political tension. The movements, for example, which demanded constitutional reform and the extension of the franchise, were partly a result of increasingly organised pressure by those who suffered in the appalling social conditions of the nineteenth-century cities. They also depended on support from the more enlightened amongst the governing classes, who realised that the modern economy demanded an evolving social outlook. Education was at the heart of the change. In theory Scotland's universities had for centuries been open to young men of ability from across the social spectrum. Free parish schools, often staffed by young graduates who were on their way to a career in the Church, prepared boys for entrance to university, and a system of bursaries eased the financial burden for some. The sons of craftsmen and even labourers do appear in the University's records: the 'lad o' pairts' did exist. For many, though, and especially those living in urban poverty, there were impenetrable barriers to access. The imperative to scrape a living overshadowed even elementary education. Only a few required higher education for their working lives, and fewer still could afford it as luxury. In this, too, change became essential.

In Edinburgh in 1821 a new institution was born, the first in Britain to have as its *raison d'être* the provision of technical education to better equip artisans and tradesmen for their occupations. Known as the 'School of Arts of Edinburgh', it was to have a distinguished history, later becoming the 'Watt Institution' (as Edinburgh's memorial to the famed inventor James Watt), then Heriot-Watt College and, from 1966, amongst the first of the new generation of technological universities: Heriot-Watt University. Soon followed by many others with similar aims throughout the country, the School of Arts of Edinburgh can be seen as the first of the mechanics' institutes, which throughout the nineteenth century provided increasingly high-level education in an ever-broadening range of technical and scientific subjects for the benefit primarily of the industrial workforce. Developing eventually into the technical college sector, the mechanics' institutes became central to the educational life of the country. Increasing social and economic pressure on the education system made it, then as now, a political issue, and it is no surprise therefore that the nineteenth century saw a raft of educational legislation that radically changed the landscape which had been comprehensively dominated for centuries by the ancient universities.

The forces for change which had had such a negative effect on eighteenth-century St Andrews clearly accelerated and deepened during the nineteenth. It would perhaps be reasonable to expect that the University's crisis might also have worsened. Broad political recognition of the need for radical overhaul of the education system, however, along with enlightened leadership within the University itself, meant that it turned the changing times to its advantage. Thus began a period of sustained growth and development. Of course, change is never achieved without pain, and the convulsions which characterised the nineteenth-century development were no exception. Throughout most of the century, a succession of government commissions analysed, challenged and reformed the education system. A major royal commission on the Universities of Scotland sat between 1826 and 1830, gathering a mass of detailed evidence about the structure, curriculum and operation of the institutions, which still forms a hugely informative source of information.

Even before the commission met, however, the wind of change was blowing. As we have seen, new subjects were appearing in the curriculum, such as Natural History, Political Economy, and English Literature (or 'Rhetoric and Belles

Resolutions

REGARDING THE DEGREES OF A.M. AND A.B.

THE UNIVERSITY OF ST. ANDREWS having abolished all the Fees hitherto exacted for the Degrees of BACHELOR and MASTER OF ARTS, the FACULTY OF ARTS consider it of the highest importance to the future success and use-fulness of the STUDENTS of the UNITED COLLEGE that they should make exemplary progress in EVERY depart-ment of their Studies, and that their attainments should be marked by the usual Academical Distinctions; and have therefore resolved to confer these distinctions in the following manner:—

1. That no Student shall be recommended by the Faculty as qualified to receive the degree of A.M. without a special examination by the Professors of Humanity, Greek, Logic, Mathematics, Moral Philosophy, Natural Philosophy, and Chemistry.

2. That the examination by the Professor of Humanity shall be, *ad aperturam*, upon the first five books of Livy,

the sixth book of the Æneid of Virgil, and Horace's Treatise de Arte Poetica.

3. That the examination by the Professor of Greek shall be, *ad aperturam*, upon the first six books of the Iliad of Homer, the Œdipus Tyrannus of Sophocles, and the seventh book of Thucydides.

4. That the examination by the Professor of Mathe-matics shall be upon the elements of Plane and Solid Geo-metry—Conic Sections—as much of Plane and Spherical Trigonometry as is sufficient for the solutions of all the cases—Algebra, in as far as regards the doctrine of Surds and the solution of Simple and Quadratic Equations—and the Elements of the Differential and Integral Cal-culus.

5. That the examination by the Professor of Natural Philosophy shall be strict upon Statics, Dynamics, and Astronomy, so far as they are taught in the Class; and shall be such as to ascertain that the Candidate has a respectable acquaintance with the leading facts and prin-ciples of the remainder of the usual course.

9. That the examination by the Professors of Logic, Moral Philosophy, and Chemistry, shall be upon the lead-ing doctrines in their respective departments; and special or strict upon such parts as they may have previously pointed out particularly to the Candidate's attention.

7. That such examinations shall be strictly private and confidential.

8. That the above examination may be divided, and

The University's Calendar for 1855, demonstrating the curricular and regulatory changes which were an important feature of the nineteenth century. (St Andrews, 1855)

Lettres', as it was then known); changes were made to tighten up the system for awarding medical degrees; new regulations were introduced to regularise examination for, and award of, the Master of Arts degree. These developments were symptomatic of an awareness within the University of a need for modernisation, and it is inevitable that there was division and conflict between the modernisers and the more moderate and conservative members of the community. One of the leading proponents of change was Thomas Chalmers, a former student of the University who in 1823 became Professor of Moral Philosophy, and who has gone down in history as the minister who led the dissenting voices out of the Church of Scotland to form the Free Church in the great Disruption of the Scottish Church in 1843.

Although daily life within the University for the average student was probab-ly much as it had been for a century or more, there was nonetheless an atmosphere of instability, which encouraged thoughts of reform, and even of revolt. For al-most two centuries, for example, the Rector of the University had been elected only by staff and senior students from amongst a small group comprising the principals of the colleges and the senior professors. In a brave move, the students in 1825 protested against this limited choice, proclaiming their choice of Rector to be none other than the enormously popular novelist Sir Walter Scott, who had

no previous connection with the institution at all. The authorities quashed the election (which in any case Scott declared himself unwilling to accept), but such a demonstration in previous generations would have been unthinkable.

That St Andrews weathered the storms of the nineteenth century is due in no small part to a succession of distinguished principals both of United College and of St Mary's College, and the high reputation of some of their other academic colleagues. The 'old order' might be said to have given way following the resignation of Professor John Lee in 1837. Lee had been Principal of the United College for less than a year, and was eminent on a wider stage both as cleric and academic, being both moderator of the General Assembly of the Church of Scotland (1844) and Principal of the University of Edinburgh (1840–59). He had been a member of the Royal Commission on the Universities and Colleges of Scotland appointed in 1826, and was thus influential in shaping the university system throughout Scotland. His tenure of the principalship in St Andrews, however, was so brief as to allow him little place in the annals of the institution, except in one unfortunately notorious respect. When he left St Andrews he seems to have taken with him a significant number of books and manuscripts from the University Library. This was a subject of some controversy even at the time, but no action was taken to recover them until some were bought at sales of his books following his death; others have subsequently come back to the library by a variety of routes. More happily, Lee is immortalised as the very first Principal of United College whose visage we know through the new and awe-inspiring medium of photography.

Lee's successor was truly an academic of international standing. David Brewster, best known today as the inventor of the kaleidoscope, was profoundly influential in the promotion of science and scientific education, and the two decades in which he steered St Andrews (1838–59) were to be crucial in its development. Some have claimed that his subsequent principalship in Edinburgh was more successful, but the controversial and at times turbulent character of his period of office in St Andrews laid the groundwork for the calmer developments led by succeeding Principals. Under his supervision important changes to the

Professor John Lee, Principal of United College in 1836–7, photographed by the St Andrews photographer Thomas Rodger, c.1850.

[Alb3-31]

Sir David Brewster, photographed
c. 1843–5 by Robert Adamson and
D.O. Hill.

[Alb24-71]

curriculum, recommended by the 1826 commissioners, were brought into effect,
and the rebuilding of the United College (begun in the 1830s) was completed,
resulting in the quadrangle which is today central to the University's North
Street site. Then as today, the reputation of an educational institution was all-
important, and several key academic appointments made during Brewster's
principalship were of great significance. In James Frederick Ferrier, for example,
who held the Chair of Moral Philosophy and Political Economy from 1845 until
his death in 1864, the University found a renowned philosopher whose first
major publication, *An Introduction to the Philosophy of Consciousness*, has been
described as 'one of the most interesting philosophical books ever written in the
English language'.

One recommendation of the 1826 commissioners, reinforced by a further commission in 1840, had been that the University's governing structure should
be comprehensively reformed. This was not put into effect, however, until the
issue was forced by an act of parliament in 1858. The Universities (Scotland) Act
significantly changed the governance of the Scottish universities; in St Andrews,
this was realised primarily by the setting up of a University Court, the fundamental purpose of which was to oversee the University's business affairs. Presided
over by the Rector (who henceforth would be elected only by the students, and in

Above: The west and north ranges of St Salvator's College, c.1846. This photograph by Robert Adamson and D.O. Hill was taken shortly before these buildings were swept away, to be replaced by the elegant quadrangle which forms the centrepiece of the University's town centre campus.

[Alb66-4]

Below: The north range of St Salvator's College quadrangle, completed in the 1840s.

[Photograph by Andrew G. Cowie, 1971; AGC-72-31]

Professor James Frederick Ferrier, photographed by Thomas Rodger, c.1855.

[Alb3-14]

a marked break from the past would not be drawn from within the University's academic population), and composed mainly of non-academic members (with representatives elected by the Senatus), the Court would 'govern' the University, taking over most of the administrative and financial work previously undertaken by the colleges, which had been severely criticised by the commissioners. This was controversial: although the Court did not become completely predominant until after later legislation, the 1858 Act nonetheless diminished the age-old autonomy of the colleges within the University. Academic matters were still to be the preserve of the Senatus which, chaired by the senior Principal, similarly increased its power, bolstering the trend towards centralisation. Another new body was the General Council, composed of the Chancellor (now reduced to a largely figurehead position), all members of the Court and the Senatus, along with all graduates. This is largely the administrative organisation of the University which remains today.

One of Brewster's main contributions to the life of St Andrews has to be his encouragement of photography. Very soon after taking up post in 1838 he founded the St Andrews Literary and Philosophical Society, a body which met regularly to engage in discussion and exploration of the intellectual advances of the day across a wide range of disciplines. Encompassing men primarily from the middle class of society, with funds and time to spend on study and experimentation, the records of the society show its engagement with natural history, palaeontology, meteorology, philosophy and a host of other subjects. Under Brewster's influence, however, a regular topic was photography. Brewster was a friend of William Henry Fox Talbot, the Wiltshire inventor who announced his discovery of a negative–positive process of 'photogenic drawing' early in 1839. One of his own primary interests being in the physics of light, Brewster picked up Talbot's discovery enthusiastically, and used the Literary and Philosophical Society as a vehicle for creating in St Andrews a 'school' of early photographers, who were to be crucial to the development of the art. Amongst this group were his friend Hugh Lyon Playfair, the Provost of St Andrews (and son of an earlier Principal of St Mary's College) and, most importantly, John Adamson, a local general practitioner and part-time lecturer in chemistry. Adamson, a leading light in St Andrews society, was secretary to the Literary and Philosophical Society, and became one of the key individuals in the development of the photographic process. The rich collection of photography left by him, his pupil and younger brother Robert (who became famous in partnership with the artist David Octavius Hill) and other photographic acolytes such as Thomas Rodger, who established a dynasty of photographers in St Andrews, is one of the greatest treasures of the modern university.

In Victorian St Andrews, Playfair was also known as a reforming Provost: in common with many Scottish towns, by the mid-nineteenth century St Andrews suffered from some appalling housing conditions, with rudimentary sanitation being responsible for outbreaks of disease which ravaged the lives of the poorer members of society. Adamson campaigned for urban improvements, many of which Playfair was able to put into effect, and it is in this period that much of the townscape of modern St Andrews came into being. Parts of the town were remodelled, slum properties were swept away and entirely new streets laid

One of the earliest photographs of St Andrews, this image of North Street was taken in 1841 or 1842 either by David Brewster or by his friend Hugh Lyon Playfair.

[Alb2-199]

Clockwise from top left:
Key players in the history
of photography:

John Adamson

[photograph by Thomas Rodger,
c.1862; Alb1-58]

Robert Adamson

[photograph by Robert Adamson
and D.O. Hill, 1844; Alb24-2-2]

Thomas Rodger

[photograph: anon., c.1855;
Alb6-32-5]

David Octavius Hill

[photograph by Thomas Rodger or
John Adamson, c.1865; Alb1-135]

Hugh Lyon Playfair

[photograph by Thomas Rodger,
c.1850; Alb6-53-3]

out, and street lighting and effective sewerage systems were installed. It is in this context of urban renewal that we have to see the improvements to the college buildings.

Brewster's successor as Principal of United College, James David Forbes, came to St Andrews from Edinburgh, where he had been Professor of Natural Philosophy. In academic terms a distinguished geologist and glaciologist, Forbes spent almost a decade in St Andrews, until his death in 1868. He was responsible for a large-scale renovation of the sadly dilapidated fifteenth-century chapel of St Salvator. One of the effects of the changes wrought by the royal commissions, and by the subsequent rebuilding of the United College, had been finally to end the custom of students living in college: no student accommodation was provided in the new buildings, the residence of students in college having for long been in decline. Initially, Forbes' attempt to resuscitate the custom by providing a small hall of residence to encourage attendance by students of high social standing was successful. One of those who lived in St Leonard's Hall was the author and anthropologist Andrew Lang, who left more than one affectionate account of St Andrews amongst his writings. Attempts to replicate the residential experiment on a larger scale, however, were a costly failure.

The demolition of the Albert Buildings in the centre of St Andrews in March 1844, documented by Dr John Adamson, for whom the event was a victory for the cause of improved sanitation.

[Alb6-156]

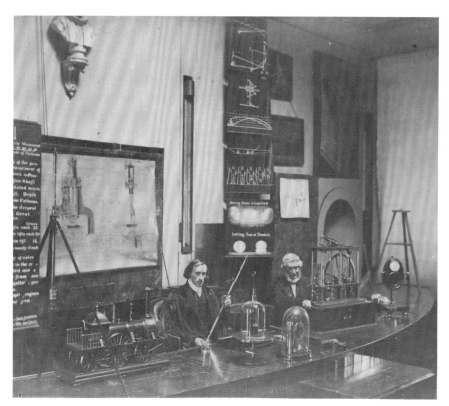

Forbes was not the senior Principal of the University. That distinction belonged to John Tulloch, who had been Principal of St Mary's College since 1854, and who thus became the senior Principal on the resignation of Brewster in 1859, a position which he retained until 1885. Tulloch, like Thomas Chalmers a decade or two earlier (although staunchly on the other side of the divide caused by the Disruption of 1843), was an eminent figure on the national Church scene, and he used his influence and his own academic and administrative abilities to enhance the position of St Mary's as an outstanding theological college central to the life of the Scottish Church. Tulloch's biography was written by his wife's friend, the Victorian novelist Margaret Oliphant, whose ghost story 'The Library Window' is a well-loved St Andrews tale. Tulloch, Ferrier and a talented group of professors throughout the University in this period ensured the reputation of the institution.

It would be misleading to portray the nineteenth century, however, as a period of unrestrained growth and development, notwithstanding the un-doubted benefits of successive decades of organisational and social change, new scientific discovery and broadening intellectual endeavour led by men of talent and reputation. As it had been throughout much of the eighteenth century, the financial situation of the University remained shaky, and student numbers fluctuated widely. In 1814 there was a bizarre proposal that the University should be moved lock, stock and barrel to Dumfries in the rural south-west of the country. How this might have improved things is difficult to understand, and very serious consideration of the proposal seems improbable. That the suggestion was made at all, however, is surely symptomatic of a real consideration in the corridors of power that the University of St Andrews might not have a sustainable future. Having grown somewhat throughout the first half of the century, student numbers remained relatively static thereafter, and even in the 1870s the number of new students arriving in the University each year rarely rose above sixty, and sometimes dropped into the thirties. This represented a very real threat to the University's continued existence. Perhaps as a consequence of the uncertainty, relationships within the University itself were not good in these decades, most notably taking the form of sometimes serious dispute between the student body and the University authorities and academic staff. This, of course, resulted in rowdy, even riotous, behaviour, which did nothing to win support for the faltering institution within the town. One has the feeling that when in the late 1860s Berry spoke of the 'resuscitation' of the University, he can have had little true idea of its current situation.

Adversity, however, can be the enemy of complacency, and once again the University survived an apparently life-threatening crisis. Building on the positive developments of the earlier nineteenth century, financial support was found (notably from the important Berry endowment, one of the gifts which enabled the struggling University to prove its financial viability), academic developments continued, and before the end of the century the foundations had been laid for the moulding of a very different institution for the twentieth century. There were two developments which, more than any others, created the modern University of St Andrews. One was the advent of higher education for women. University education had been the exclusive preserve of males since the middle ages. When in 1862, without precedent, a female student matriculated for study, it represented a huge challenge to the established order. Elizabeth Garrett, later to become the first qualified female medical doctor in Britain, was well ahead of her time, however. In the ensuing rumpus, her matriculation was quashed by the Senatus, her signature scored out of the matriculation register, and entrance to the University denied. She thus failed to obtain her education in St Andrews, and studied instead at home in London, passing the examination of the Society of Apothecaries (which entitled her to practise medicine), and later in the University of Paris, from which she gained an MD degree. Founder of the New Hospital for Women in London, she went on to be involved also in the foundation of the London School of Medicine for Women, subsequently becoming its dean. Later in life she became England's first female mayor. A powerful advocate for the movement leading towards women's suffrage, Garrett had raised the issue of education for women at St Andrews, which was to be the cause of significant dispute for some years to come.

Right: Elizabeth Garrett (later Anderson), whose attempt to matriculate as a medical student in 1862 was rejected by the University Senatus.

[Photograph by John Adamson, 1862–3; Alb8-40]

Below right: The Matriculation Register, showing Garrett's signature, lightly scored through in pencil by the University's clerk.

[UYUY309]

Garrett was not without her supporters amongst the academic staff, and the fact that they lost the argument in 1862 did not imply that the matter was dead and buried. Largely at the instigation of William Knight, Professor of Moral Philosophy, in 1877 a scheme was successfully introduced to allow women to benefit from university education whilst avoiding the controversial business of their having to enter the University and mix with the male students. In effect a form of distance learning, the 'Lady Literate in Arts' (LLA) programme offered courses equivalent to university level in a range of disciplines.

It was the responsibility of the student to prepare herself, often through other distance learning schemes, such as the St George's Hall Correspondence Class in Edinburgh, before being examined at local centres throughout the UK (and eventually throughout the world). A visionary scheme, it was phenomenally well-subscribed, eventually delivering the qualification to over 5,000 women out of the almost 28,000 who passed in one or more subjects. Remaining popular for almost three decades after the eventual admission of women to full-time study, the LLA continued in operation until 1931.

On one level it is possible to view the LLA in a cynical light: it was undoubtedly a money-spinner which used the demand for female education to enhance the coffers, whilst managing to keep women at arm's length from the institution. It is also true that the revenue, and perhaps the reputation, earned from the LLA scheme was important in helping to rebuild the flagging fortunes of the University in a time of crisis. The complete story is, of course, more complex. Records of the discussions surrounding the institution of the LLA show that there was real concern amongst its promoters to engage the University in the process of broader social change which would lead, eventually, to the improvement of women's status in British society, and to the granting of the female vote in the early years of the twentieth century. That the LLA was so popular demonstrates that it met a significant demand; that it helped to save the University as well should hardly be a reason for criticism. The contemporary position of the Watt Institution in Edinburgh provides a useful comparison. Similarly struggling to attract enough students to secure its future, the governors in 1869 eventually acceded to long-standing demands from women for access to its courses. This was

Below left: The Calendar, which details the 1891 syllabus and the previous year's results, for the hugely successful 'distance learning' course for women, the LLA.

[St Andrews, 1890]

Below right: An LLA class certificate, awarded to Frances Hill for Geography and French in 1903.

[UYUY377]

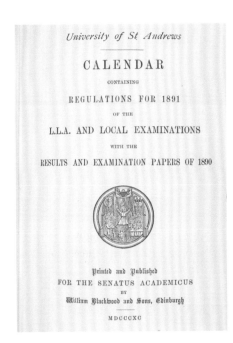

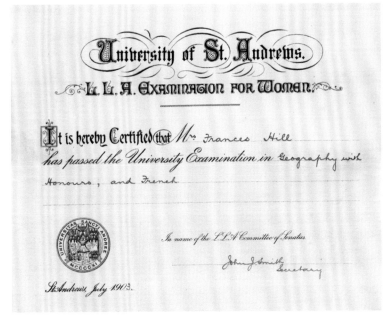

a controversial move which had been opposed for some time, but the governors eventually gave in, stating that they could not find any actual rule within the college's constitution which forbade it. St Andrews was by nature a more conservative institution, and came to a more limited solution to the immediate problem. However, that solution paved the way for more profound change.

Women were finally admitted to full-time study in St Andrews in 1892, formal authority to do so having been granted to the universities by an ordinance made under the terms of an act of parliament in 1889. In 1896, substantially funded by the proceeds of the LLA, a newly constructed 'University Hall of Residence for Women Students' was opened, the first female university residence in Scotland. Within a few years it had to be extended because the demand for places was so great. In St Andrews, the early matriculation of women considerably outstripped other Scottish universities. The pre-existing involvement of women at St Andrews may well be responsible for this, both through the LLA and through the institution of 'Local Examinations' which prepared potential entrants to a higher standard than previously. These examinations were inclusive of women candidates from the beginning, who were thus fitted not only for the LLA, but also for matriculation, as soon as the gender barrier was lifted.

In a broad context, the admission of women to study in the country's universities was to have a fundamental impact on society, and in the short term it

University Hall, the first female university residence in Scotland, photographed shortly after completion.

[Photograph by J. Valentine & Co.; JV-30377]

was an important step towards the enfranchisement of women. Following an intense and increasingly violent national campaign (during which, in June 1913, the University's marine laboratory was the subject of an arson attack), in 1918 the first women allowed to vote in Britain were those over thirty years of age who were householders, the spouses of householders, or who held university degrees. It was a decade later before legislation was passed allowing voting equality with men. As with the Watt Institution in 1869, the admission of women to full-time study opened up the University to a lucrative new market, provided a radical and welcome increase in student numbers, and led in the longer term to a gradual extension of the range and number of courses offered. The changing nature of the institution in turn attracted yet more students, and ensured its long-term viability.

This very hazy photograph, from a personal album compiled by William Carmichael McIntosh who, as Professor of Natural History, was in charge of the marine laboratory destroyed by a suffragette arson attack, shows a 'votes for women' demonstration in June 1913.

[ms37102/12/48r/2]

A very early cohort of women students, photographed in St Salvator's quadrangle. The woman seated on the far left of the step is perhaps Agnes Blackadder, who in 1895 was the first female graduate of the University.

[Group1896-4a]

The first female graduate, who gained her MA in March 1895, was Agnes Blackadder. She subsequently studied medicine in Queen Margaret College for Women (part of the University of Glasgow), and went on to an eminent career as a consultant dermatologist in a London hospital. During the First World War she set up the radiography unit in the Scottish Women's Hospital at Royaumont in France. Having led a life which was pioneering in many ways, she died in 1964. In today's University, where female students outnumber males, it is extraordinary to consider that our very first female graduate died only fifty years ago.

The other crucial, and equally contentious, development of the later nineteenth century was the establishment of University College, Dundee. It took about a decade of argument, discussion and searching for funds to achieve it, but in 1881, with significant private funding provided by the Baxter family of Dundee, a college was founded there, offering a broad range of subjects. Although established independently, it had been explicit from the beginning that it would seek some sort of formal relationship with a university – most logically with St Andrews. From early days, the two institutions co-operated, and Dundee students could gain degrees from St Andrews without having studied there. It was not until shortly after the Universities (Scotland) Act of 1889, however, that the two institutions finally reached agreement to unite, and University College, Dundee became a constituent college of the University of St Andrews; it is worth noting that this event was very probably a further nail in the coffin of male-only education in St Andrews, since from its foundation University College was co-educational. The relationship of the new college with the University was at times to be difficult, but it was another example of the visionary approach of the later nineteenth-century leaders of the University, often pursued in the face of significant opposition: the University grew its way out of recession, rather than allowing itself to shrink yet further, the result of which would have been inevitable oblivion.

Above left: Far left, Principal Donaldson, somewhat over-shadowed by the imposing figure of the Rector, the 3rd marquis of Bute. Detail from a group photograph taken in 1895 at an unidentified University ceremony.

[Group1895-3a]

Above right: The early buildings of University College, Dundee, on the Nethergate, photographed in the early 1950s.

[Anon., by kind permission of University of Dundee Archive Services; CMS 1/1/27]

The figure overwhelmingly responsible for the successes of this period was James Donaldson, Principal of United College (and senior Principal) from 1886, and indeed the first Principal of the University under a renewed constitution from 1890. It is testament to the pace of social, economic and industrial change in the latter half of the nineteenth century that another royal commission was appointed in 1876 to investigate the universities and their effectiveness in meeting current demand. The resulting Universities (Scotland) Act of 1889 made further significant changes to both the constitutional organisation (further strengthening the Court) and the curriculum, more positively embedding science within the core teaching of the University. Although the degree of Bachelor of Science had been instituted in 1876, one of the developments enabled by the 1889 Act was the adoption of a series of ordinances regulating science degrees, and eventually the creation of a separate Faculty of Science in 1897.

Due to these developments, the institution saw considerable growth in the later nineteenth century. As the curriculum expanded and modernised, especially in science, so new buildings were erected. The intellectual development of the institution was reflected in its physical growth, again within the context of a significant expansion of the town itself. Flourishing largely as a result of the industrial success of Dundee, St Andrews saw much new building in this period, as wealthy businessmen chose to invest their funds in grandiose residences built in a cleaner environment removed from the city. It was one of these fine residences, on the Scores, which the University purchased (largely with funds from the Berry bequest) as the official residence of the Principal. Apart from a few years as home to one of the University's academic schools, it has remained the official residence of the incumbent Principal ever since. As ever, the fortunes of University and town went hand in hand; from the decline of the eighteenth century, the close interdependence of town and gown ensured that the new-found

The Bute Medical Building, completed in 1899, thanks to a generous benefaction by the 3rd marquis of Bute.

[Photograph by George M Cowie, April 1950; GMC-FB74a]

prosperity benefited them both equally. With significant support from several wealthy benefactors, as well as the extensions to the library and provision for the first time of adequate sports facilities, new buildings for Medicine and Natural Science, Natural History and Chemistry were erected in St Andrews. There were similarly extensive developments, especially for the sciences and engineering, in Dundee, where the new University College was growing at a remarkable rate.

When George Walker and Alexander Berry walked into St Andrews for the first time in 1796, their daily lives would have had more in common with students of the fifteenth or sixteenth century than those of the twenty-first. The University was larger than in its earlier days; the curriculum was broader and teaching methods had changed, but it was still in some respects a medieval institution in a medieval town. The students' diet, the nature of their accommodation, their need to study by candle-light – all these things belonged to the past, not to the future. In contrast, the student arriving in St Andrews (probably by train) just over a century later would have a very different experience. Twenty-four new students signed the matriculation register on the same day as Walker and Berry in 1797. On the equivalent day a century later it was signed by seventy-five new students, a third of whom were women. The students, who would be taught not only by professors but by a staff greatly enlarged by lecturers and assistants, chose specialist courses across a wide range of arts and science disciplines, rather than undertaking the standard 'one-size-fits-all' arts curriculum. They could benefit from the facilities of a students' union building, and the efforts of a formally constituted Student Representative Council. There were new buildings, some of which were supplied with electric lighting, and even the telephone was making its appearance. Less obvious to the innocent bystander, the University was, thanks mainly to the activities of the nineteenth-century commissions, governed in a completely different way, and was part of a modern system of education controlled and funded by government as never before. Indeed, in the University as in the rest of society, the world had changed beyond all recognition.

Right: A Chemistry laboratory in University College, Dundee, photographed in 1888.

[Anon., by kind permission of University of Dundee Archive Services; CMS 1/1/77]

Below: Looking west along The Scores, one of St Andrews' new 'suburbs' developed in the late nineteenth century, photographed c.1915 by J. Valentine & Co.

[JV-81186]

THE SCORES, ST. ANDREWS

7 Conflict and growth

In the weeks and days leading up to 31 December 1999 the international press bustled with analysis of the passing century and with speculation about the century to come. As midnight struck in time-zones around the world, communities and countries outshone each other in the lavishness of their celebrations – firework displays and pageants were followed by a truly global audience. Poised between the thrill of belonging to a moment in history and the fear of chaos should computer systems choke on the 'millennium bug', millions of people were caught up in an event which, curiously, would make absolutely no difference to their lives.

Members of Tongan church choirs, in traditional dress, watch the very first firework display celebrating the incoming millennium on 1 January 2000.

[Photograph by David Gray, ©Reuters; by kind permission of Reuters/Corbis]

As 1899 turned to 1900, though a centennial event rather than a millennial moment, it might be expected that people would have been similarly moved to celebrate. However, leading up to the year's end, the local St Andrews press carried virtually no reference to the New Year festival. A relatively sombre review of the past year appeared, but there was no mention of any communal festivities or celebrations. One letter politely chastised those who spoke of the century ending in 1899 rather than in 1900, but even in the following year there was apparently no major celebration. Indeed, St Andrews Town Council decreed that New Year's Day 1901 was not even a public holiday, since, being a Tuesday, it was a market day. One local community reported with apparent satisfaction that Hogmanay had passed off peacefully, with 'first-footing' being happily rare – a far cry from the modern stereotype of the 'traditional' Scottish New Year! We could conclude that the 'tradition' owes a great deal to an increasingly manipulative marketing industry. But other reasons can be found to account for the subdued birth of the twentieth century. In the last edition of 1899, the *St Andrews Citizen* published an editorial in which it rather apologetically excused itself for wishing its readers a happy New Year, at a time when many people refused even to send Christmas cards out of respect for those who mourned the loss of loved ones killed in the second Anglo-Boer war. Newspaper reports generally in this period support the idea that there was a pervading sense of gloom in the country which discouraged overt celebration.

The somewhat apologetic New Year greeting published by the *St Andrews Citizen* on 30 December 1899.

[per AN4.S2C5]

Though locally, as nationally, the mood was despondent, there was some cause for optimism. St Andrews was expanding: in 1851 its population had been just over 5,000; by 1901 it had increased by 50 per cent to 7,621, a rate of growth almost exactly mirroring that of other significant towns in the area, such as Cupar. The architectural development of the town begun in the later nineteenth century was to continue into the early years of the twentieth. Interestingly, however, it seems that the number of houses in which this rising population was accommodated had grown by less than 20 per cent (about 250), a figure which reinforces our impressions of overcrowding in nineteenth-century towns: it seems that whilst wealthy industrialists accommodated themselves in new, large houses around the periphery of the town, increasing numbers of ordinary folk crowded into the historic centre.

Health statistics, on the other hand, seem to indicate that in some respects life was nonetheless improving for all. The urban improvements of the nineteenth century, as well as medical progress, did have a long-term impact on the welfare of the population: the death rate had dropped from 18.2 per 1,000 in 1855 to 14.1 per 1,000 in 1900. In particular, the rampant diseases which cruelly affected the young population had declined in their severity. Although still appalling by twenty-first century standards, the diseases which annually would kill around thirty St Andrews children before their fifth birthday (around 33 per cent of all deaths) in mid-nineteenth century St Andrews claimed just over twenty (22.6 per cent of all deaths, from a lower death rate within a greatly increased population) in 1900. Of those, several were due to prematurity or other birth complications, and it is surprising that in that year, although a few cases were treated, no children lost their lives in St Andrews to the notoriously dangerous diphtheria. The most common fatal diseases amongst the child population were the still familiar, although now less deadly, whooping cough and measles. Cholera and other 'zymotic' diseases of which Dr John Adamson had so complained in the early 1860s had almost entirely disappeared from the populace by 1900. Sanitation and the quality of housing had greatly improved (although even in 1900 the Medical Officer of Health was recommending the demolition or closing up of a few insanitary properties), and the citizens of the city now had access to a hospital, opened in the 1870s.

Street lighting brightened the town; public entertainments were more common and more varied; the iron fist of the Kirk, which for centuries had taken a restrictive view of public morality, loosened its grip somewhat; communications with the outside world by road, rail and even telephone, were steadily improving, and the motor car was beginning to insinuate itself into ordinary lives, bringing increasing numbers of tourists – holidaymakers and day-trippers – to the town to enjoy the beaches, the historic environment and, of course, the golf courses. Grand new hotel buildings transformed the skyline. Life in early twentieth century St Andrews would have been more recognisable to a citizen of a century later than to one of a century earlier.

Opposite above: The new St Andrews Memorial Hospital on its opening day, 27 August 1902. This replaced the town's first hospital, which had been opened in a building in Abbotsford Place in 1875.

[Photograph by John Fairweather; GMC-F14]

Opposite below: St Andrews' magnificent beaches were a key element in the growing tourist trade of the late nineteenth and early twentieth centuries. This photograph was taken on the west sands c.1900.

[Photograph by John Fairweather; GMC-F59]

St Andrews continued to draw
tourists throughout the twentieth
century. Kinkell Braes caravan
park was one of many founded
across the country after the Second
World War, as car ownership
increased and caravanning offered
the possibility of budget holidays.

[Photograph by J. Valentine & Co.,
1955; JV-D485]

In the session ending in September 1900 the University had a student population of 406 served by a staff of around 75 professors, lecturers and assistants. Roughly one third of the students and staff were based not in St Andrews, but in University College, Dundee. Between the two campuses, a staggering variety of subjects was offered, ranging from the traditional arts curriculum incorporating such disciplines as Latin and Greek, Logic and Mathematics, to the more up-to-date Modern Languages, Political Economy, Engineering, various specialist branches of Medicine, and Jurisprudence. Although still based almost entirely in the medieval centre of the town, the St Andrews part of the operation had grown significantly in its estate.

Perhaps the zenith of the distinguished career of Principal Donaldson was the celebration of the University's quincentenary, which was held in September 1911. If the populace as a whole had disdained to celebrate the turning of the century, the University had no intention of failing to highlight its own marked antiquity. (There is, however, no indication in the records of previous centenaries having been noted in any way.) The choice of date is interesting, since the key dates in the foundation process may be said to have been 1410, 1412 and 1414. The records do not explain how it was arrived at, but it may not be unconnected with the twenty-fifth anniversary of Donaldson's principalship. The planning having been in progress for three years, the celebration required the construction of a temporary hall capable of seating 3,500 people, to accommodate the invited throng.

As with modern celebrations, there was a fundraising element to the occasion. The costs were largely defrayed by subscription, and the event earned for the University a founding donation to a fund which would later provide a permanent graduation venue – the Younger Hall which still sits on North Street. An opening reception was hosted by the Chancellor, and the scene was described in the press as of 'probably unequalled brilliance in the annals of the University', with the colours of academic dress reminiscent of 'the riot of colour in Dutch tulip fields in early summer'. Following a wonderful sunset, male students held a torchlight procession on the evening of 12 September. On the following morning an impressive procession of members of the University and the many invited delegates was led past thousands of onlookers by the band of the Scots Guards, wending its way slowly from United College to the parish church in the town centre, where a commemorative service was held. In the afternoon, there was a ceremony at which the representatives of no fewer than 145 universities and learned societies (led by a papal nuncio delivering congratulations on behalf of the pontiff) presented congratulatory scrolls to the Chancellor, who gave an official address to the 3,573 people present. The official guest list was glittering: many of the most eminent figures of the country attended, and were provided with personal hospitality at a great many distinguished homes across the north and east of Fife. It has to be admitted, however, that the appeal of the event was apparently not sufficient to persuade the King or the archbishops of York and Canterbury to accept their invitations. In the evening, historical tableaux were staged by students at which a variety of scenes from the University's past were depicted, and a student symposium was held.

On Thursday 13 September 1911 an impressive procession of dignitaries from Scottish towns, other universities and members of the University of St Andrews (including the Chancellor, Lord Balfour of Burleigh, shown here) assembled in the quadrangle and wound its way through the town to Holy Trinity Church for a service to commemorate the institution's 500th anniversary.

[Photograph by A C Robertson, UYUY185/2/8/52/3]

One of the 145 commemorative scrolls which were presented to the University by invited representatives of other institutions at a special quincentenary ceremony on 13 September 1911. This one was given by the Dundee Chamber of Commerce.

[UYUY185]

The Dundee Chamber of Commerce begs the ancient and famous University of St Andrews to accept its respectful and sincere greetings and its most cordial congratulations on the celebration of the five hundredth anniversary of the foundation of the University.

While even in the higher spheres of Commerce a University Degree is not generally considered a necessary part of the equipment for the battle of life, yet the Dundee Chamber of Commerce acknowledges the high value of an academic education for merchants. Many of its members, past and present, have been University Graduates, and not a few of these cherish with pride the privilege of calling the far famed University of St Andrews their Alma Mater. The Chamber therefore gladly welcomes every opportunity of drawing closer the bonds of Union which already exist between St Andrews and Dundee; one reflects the lustre of the renowned and venerable Mother University, the other harbours University College, her thriving daughter.

The Dundee Chamber of Commerce wishes to thank the University of St Andrews most heartily for the signal honour conferred upon it by the University, in inviting its President to assist at this celebration as the Delegate of the Chamber, and it avails itself, with much gratification, of this opportunity to assure the University of its profound respect and devotion. May the ancient Centre of learning in the Grey City by the Sea continue to prosper, to expand and to flourish, for the spread of knowledge and the enlightenment of Mankind.

Dundee 7th September 1911.

R. Black   President

James Cunningham   Vice-president

William Mackenzie   Ex-president

Geo. C. Keiller   Secretary

The third day of celebration saw a large-scale ceremony at which no fewer than 100 honorary degrees were bestowed and the new Rector was installed, followed in the afternoon by garden parties. Later a lavish banquet was attended by 527 individuals – all male, the 'Ladies Committee' having agreed that the accommodation was too limited for the ladies to attend – held in the University's new Bell Pettigrew Museum, which was formally opened during the evening's proceedings. Friday 15th was a day especially devoted to celebrations in Dundee, which took the form of receptions, addresses, a formal lunch and excursions to a variety of places of interest. The evening in St Andrews saw a dinner for graduates and students, and a student ball – at which, according to a press report, the music and dancing were excellent, but the catering 'meagre'! The celebrations were hailed as a great success and a 'judicious mixture of the academic and the festive', a description which perhaps accords with Bower's portrayal of the scenes of both pomp and informal festivity which accompanied the arrival of the papal bulls in St Andrews almost 500 years earlier. Donaldson must have been well pleased with the result of his planning and exertion; in his eightieth year, his packed schedule (including personally hosting in University House several eminent visitors, one of whom was Andrew Carnegie) must have been very demanding, but there is no doubt that the event significantly raised the profile of the University both nationally and internationally.

Within a few years, however, the jubilance and optimism of 1911 were to be dashed by events taking place far from St Andrews. Donaldson lived only just long enough to see the outbreak of the First World War. Its effect can be seen most obviously in the immediate decline of the student population, as the country's youth was mobilised to play its part in the horrors of trench warfare. The 510 matriculated students of session 1912/13 dropped to 428 in 1914/15, and to 361 in the following year. Almost 1,000 individuals, graduates and current students of the University along with some fifty of its staff, served in the war, predominantly as commissioned officers. Over half had been members of either the University's Company of Artillery Volunteers or its Officer Training Corps. Many served with great distinction, being mentioned in despatches and even decorated for their bravery. Of those who served, 130 died in or as a direct result of action; many more were prisoners of war, were seriously wounded, or suffered from illness derived from their war experience. If there had been an atmosphere of gloom at the turn of the century because of the warfare in South Africa, it

The Bell Pettigrew museum, founded in memory of James Bell Pettigrew (1834–1908), Chandos Professor of Medicine and Anatomy from 1875 to 1908, which was formally opened during the quincentenary celebrations of 1911. The collections had been started by the Literary and Philosophical Society of St Andrews, founded by Sir David Brewster in 1838, and were transferred to the University in 1904.

[Anon.; StAU-BPMus-1]

is difficult to imagine the community's feelings when the war experience was so magnified, and came so very close to home for so many people.

The role of the universities in warfare, then as now, was crucial in more ways than the provision of fighting men: not all of those listed in the Roll of Service fought. Percy Herring, the Professor of Physiology, served as a medical practitioner for the returning injured, in his case at Stobhill Hospital in Glasgow. He was also a member of the 'Chemical Warfare Committee'. Several of his academic colleagues and their former students served in other hospitals, including the Dundee War Hospital. Others served in medical capacities in the field, including Reginald Barrow, an ophthalmic surgeon with the Indian Expeditionary Force, and Adeline Campbell, a surgeon in the Scottish Women's Hospital in Serbia, one of several women from the University who worked there in varying capacities. Another student, Agnes Hodge, nursed in military hospitals in France, and Donald Forbes became a surgeon in the Royal Naval Reserve. The role of the very first female graduate of the University, Agnes Blackadder, in the Scottish Women's Hospital at Royaumont has already been mentioned. Several graduates acted as chaplains to the forces in the field. One of Herring's assistant lecturers, James Hewitt, was a 'Chemical Adviser' in both the Southern and Western military command. Arnold Gibson, Professor of Engineering, served within the Royal Aircraft Establishment as Officer in Charge of aero-engine research. A lecturer in English literature, James Roy, served as an intelligence officer, and was a member of the British mission to Poland, Hungary and Czechoslovakia.

We can speculate that the absence of so many of the University's students and staff, and the regular news of casualties and fatalities, would have changed the character and mood of the institution. There must also have been a constant reminder of the situation through the necessary reorganisation of classes and the rescheduling of examinations to facilitate the studies of those who lived constantly awaiting call-up. The urgent need for medical staff also prompted an increase in the number of medical students, particularly women, passing through the University. In addition, the nature of some of the work going on within the University's workshops and laboratories was overtly related to the war effort. Primarily under the leadership of James Irvine, an eminent organic chemist who had become Professor of Chemistry in the United College in 1909, and who would become Principal of the University in 1921, the chemistry laboratories turned their efforts to the development and production of anaesthetics, methods for the treatment of both tetanus and meningitis, and other materials required for military purposes. Under the direction of Professor Herring the laboratories of the Bute Medical School also undertook important research into military gases, including mustard gas, used with such devastating effects during the war. Although it is not entirely clear, there does also seem to be some evidence that the engineering workshops in University College, Dundee were turned over to the production of munitions during the war.

The emotion which surrounded the position of the University in relation to the war is perhaps exemplified by the students' election, in 1916, of none other than Field Marshall Douglas Haig as their new Rector. He was, of course, unable immediately to take up his rectorial duties, and was not installed until the end of the war. That the students made such a choice, however, is telling of their attitude. Haig's connection with the University did not end there; his personal chaplain for part of the war was George Duncan, who in its aftermath took up post as Professor of Divinity and Biblical Criticism, and from 1922 to 1928 Haig served the University as its Chancellor. Interestingly, too, it is a mark of the tenor of the times that a Senatus committee tasked with looking at the issue of military training of students came up with a report in 1915, which stated that:

The Senatus believing that Military Training is beneficial to students, that it does not interfere with academic work, that due preparation in time of peace for the defence of the Country is the duty of every citizen and recognising the great value of the services which University students trained in the Officers Training Corps have been enabled to render as Officers in the Army, resolves that no male student of the University who is a native of the United Kingdom, except those who are physically unfit or over thirty years of age, shall be eligible for graduation in Arts, Science or Medicine unless he has undergone a minimum amount of military training recognised as adequate by the University: due consideration and relaxation being given to all special cases.

From the right, Field Marshall Douglas Haig, elected Rector in 1916, in the grounds of University House with his successor as Rector, the celebrated author James Barrie, Principal Irvine, and Sir James Younger of Mount Melville. The photograph was taken on the occasion of Barrie's installation as Rector, on 3 May 1922.

[Photograph by Central News Ltd, London; Group1922-1]

Principal Donaldson must have been saddened in the closing years of his life to see the institution, which he had worked so hard to build up, so sadly depleted. He did not live to see it revive after the war, since on 9 March 1915, still in office at the age of eighty-four (and only a couple of weeks after he chaired his last meeting of the University Court), he died peacefully in University House. His death undoubtedly deprived the University of a great leader who for almost thirty years had overseen a period of remarkable growth and development, and whose period of office had seen such colossal change in the nature of the higher education system. The sense of loss sustained by the University, and the nature of the period in which he had held office, is made very clear by the official tribute to him enshrined within the minutes of the University Senatus.

> *The Senatus desire to place on record an expression of the great grief and sense of bereavement they have sustained through the death of Principal Sir James Donaldson . . . He came to St Andrews as Principal of the United College in the year 1886, and most of the members of the Senatus have known no other Vice-Chancellor of the University.*

> *The twenty-nine years during which Sir James Donaldson held his high office have been a period unexampled in the history of all the Universities of Scotland for the rapid growth and large expansion they have witnessed. Of this growth the late Principal was to a large extent the promoter, and as head of this the oldest Scottish University he was quick to take advantage of it. To the period of his principalship belong not only the great development of the University under the Act of 1889, but also the addition to the University of University College, Dundee, the admission of women to University classes and degrees, and the founding of the Carnegie Trust, which has done so much to improve the lot of the students . . . Thus it has come about that many subjects are now taught in the University, which at the beginning of the late Principal's administration were not thought of, and that the number of the staff has been multiplied many times. The part the late Principal took in encouraging and directing these manifold enrichments of the University life of St Andrews may never be precisely known but was unquestionably large.*

> *The Principal was singularly fitted by his gifts and character to be the head of a University in such a period of rapid growth. He possessed an unrivalled knowledge of the educational systems of various nations and periods, and an unfailing sympathy with the young which gave him a profound and simple insight into the true nature of education. All who were engaged in the great work of education saw in him their friend, and he was in constant touch with teachers of every grade. He also found ready access to the ears of statesmen and administrators . . .*

Donaldson had been held in equal esteem well beyond St Andrews: the University received a personal letter of condolence from the then prime minister, Lord Asquith, who lamented the passing of his old friend. Quite aside from his great contribution to the life and development of the University, a long-lasting bequest from Donaldson was that of his library and papers. A noted classicist and writer on religious history, his many books and voluminous correspondence are still a resource of significance to the University Library's research holdings.

His successor, John Herkless, was appointed less than a month after Donaldson's death, having been a respected Professor of Ecclesiastical History in St Mary's College since 1894. The haste with which he was appointed makes it seem possible that the succession had been decided in advance: Donaldson's health had been failing for some time, and his demise cannot have come as a surprise. Under the old system, before the advent of the post of 'Principal of the

The cathedral and 'leaning' bell-tower of Pisa, in a photograph from one of the impressive albums compiled by Principal Donaldson on his frequent travels in Britain and Europe.

[ms29951/7/37]

University', Herkless would have been regarded automatically as the 'senior principal' following Donaldson's death, and it is easy to assume that, despite the new formal arrangements, the University continued for the time being to follow its previous custom. The local newspaper mentioned the names of some possible candidates for the post within the context of its obituary of Donaldson, and anecdote places D'Arcy Wentworth Thompson, then Professor of Natural History in University College, Dundee, in the frame. There seems, however, to be no record within the University's own archives of any competition for the post. It is possible that under Herkless there might have been strides forward in the area of town-gown relationships, since he was also active on the local stage, having been elected Provost of St Andrews in 1911. He did not long outlive the stringencies of the war years, however, dying without having been able to make his mark in any lasting way, after only five years in office.

At the end of the war the return of demobilised servicemen, combined with the 'natural' intake of new students, saw numbers rise sharply, particularly in medical subjects. In the immediate post-war years, too, new subjects were introduced to the curriculum to keep pace with increasing technological advance. The new course in aero-engineering to be taught in Dundee, for example, is an obvious development stemming from the technology of warfare. With increasing numbers and the euphoria of the post-war period, characterised by the firm belief that there could never again be warfare on this scale, the mood in the town and University was of confidence in a brightening future.

The premature death of Principal Herkless in 1920 saw the appointment as his successor of James Irvine, who took up office early in the following year. Like Donaldson, Irvine (who was knighted in 1925) oversaw the University for just over three decades, in a period characterised by turbulent change, expansion and modernisation. Irvine, who had studied and taught both in the University and abroad since the later years of the previous century, was a man already steeped in the culture and traditions of St Andrews when he assumed office. It is difficult to separate the story of the developments of the ensuing thirty years from Irvine's personality and his deeply held ambitions for the institution. Eminent as a chemist in both peacetime and wartime, his academic reputation was already international.

Irvine's preoccupations as Principal are made manifest by a glance along the shelves of his papers, still arranged within the University Archives in the order in which he kept them. The file titles include names of individuals who were already, or would become, well known as benefactors of the University, emphasising the tireless work he undertook to solidify the financial position, and his realisation that the modern University required substantial injection of private funds in order to invest in its infrastructure. Not only did Irvine successfully procure several large donations, but he laid the groundwork for the University's increasing dependence on support from its alumni, by establishing the Alumnus Association in 1926. 'American Universities' is another file title: if St Andrews was to succeed,

Principal Sir James Irvine, in a photograph taken by the London portrait studio of Bassano Ltd., c.1925.

[GPS]

it must have a truly international outlook and offer an educational experience of international quality.

To that end, Irvine was a frequent visitor to the USA, studying American models of education and spreading the word about St Andrews. His concern to improve the amenities of the University is shown in files on athletics and the gymnasium, student residences and the University chapel: his period in office saw the building of the new graduation hall on North Street, principally funded by Viscount Younger of Mount Melville, and the provision both of a new residence, St Salvator's Hall, and a large-scale refurbishment of the fifteenth-century St Salvator's chapel. These latter two projects were funded mainly by the generous benefactions of Irvine's American friend Edward Harkness, and were part of Irvine's aim to recreate the atmosphere, long since lost in St Andrews, of a collegiate university. Earlier, in 1921, a small residence for male students, Chattan House, had been opened. The aim of increasing residential opportunity was furthered again in 1930 with the opening of St Salvator's Hall to provide additional accommodation for men, and the subsequent extension and re-modelling of Chattan House, re-opened in 1939 with the adjoining McIntosh Hall (a building gifted by Professor W.C. McIntosh) as an additional women's residence. For much of the twentieth century St Andrews remained distinctive amongst the ancient Scottish universities for its generous provision of student residence. Irvine's policy of extending the advantages of higher education to a

The Younger Hall, at the heart of the University, is used for ceremonies, examinations, concerts and other events, and is the home of the modern University's Music Centre. It was opened in June 1929 by the Duchess of York, later Queen Elizabeth.

[Anon., c. 1950; StA-YoungH-1]

broader cross-section of the population appears through work on adult education, bursaries and scholarships. The range of subjects continued to expand, and with it the student numbers, until in the early 1930s there were consistently over 1,000 students in the University, with roughly a third of them women.

The atmosphere of St Andrews in this period must have been exciting. As well as a growing university, the town was home to a thriving cultural scene. It was one of the centres of a resurgence of interest in Scottish identity, and indeed political nationalism, which emerged in the 1930s. Much of the activity in St Andrews revolved around the Abbey Bookshop in South Street, whose owner, the American James Whyte, acted as the catalyst for much of the literary and artistic flourishing. A noted benefactor of the arts, and close to such cultural icons as Christopher Murray Grieve (better known as Hugh McDiarmid), the poet Edwin Muir and his writer wife Willa, and the composer Francis George Scott, Whyte deliberately tried to foster St Andrews as a hub of Scottish cultural renaissance. Returning from lengthy travels in continental Europe, Edwin and Willa Muir settled in St Andrews for several years from 1935 (living in a house rented from Whyte), and it is to Willa's literary portrait of her life with Edwin, *Belonging:A Memoir*, that we owe much of our knowledge of this period in St Andrews. She was a graduate of the University, having taken a first-class honours degree in Classics in 1910, and was probably the driving force behind the couple's many celebrated translations of modern European novels. Despite their obvious talents

Opposite: St Salvator's Hall, first opened in 1930.

Right: The Editing Committee of the student magazine *College Echoes*, 1910–11. Top left is Miss Wilhelmina Anderson who, using her married name, became the celebrated writer Willa Muir.

[Group1911-89-n]

and celebrity in literary circles, to its detriment the University did not offer either of them employment, and after some years they left the town, with a less than enthusiastic attitude towards it. For a time, however, the students living in St Andrews were fortunate indeed to be in such a fertile cultural environment.

The population of United College and St Mary's (which in the period was very small, rarely exceeding thirty students, who at the time were all postgraduate candidates for the ministry) still outstripped that of University College, Dundee, but not by much. Roughly 60 per cent of the students studied in St Andrews, but the increasing popularity of the Conjoint Medical School (founded in 1898) and the Dental School (founded in 1916 within the new Dundee Dental hospital), meant that the Dundee campus of the University was rapidly catching up: by the late 1930s the student population was split more or less equally between the two locations.

The outbreak of the Second World War in 1939 came at a time of marked progress in the University. Student numbers had risen, new subjects were firmly embedded in the curriculum, and the future perhaps looked more certain than it had done for some time. War again disrupted the studies of many students, but government policy encouraged the university sector to continue its activities largely unhindered, and there was less requisitioning of university facilities. The contribution of staff and students to the war effort was no less than had been the case in 1914-18: the Roll of Service lists approximately 2,000 staff, students and alumni who served in the armed forces in a full-time capacity. The death toll was proportionately lower than in the earlier war, reflecting the nature of the warfare, with rather less than 10 per cent losing their lives. The photographs in the Roll of Honour, however – one of them Principal Irvine's own son, drowned on naval service in 1944 – provide the same tragic litany of young lives cut short. The provision of short-term training courses for the armed forces saw an influx of temporary students during the war years, including significant numbers of Polish students. As had been the case after 1918, there was a marked post-war bulge as students returned to complete courses which had been interrupted by military service. Whilst graduation figures dipped a little in the central years of the war, therefore, overall student numbers remained largely unaffected, and indeed grew marginally over these years.

The issue which most affected the University for much of the first half of the twentieth century finds eloquent expression in the title of Irvine's file on the subject: 'The Dundee problem'. The relationship between the Dundee and the St Andrews arms of the institution was a constant source of vexation. When University College joined St Andrews in 1890, duplicated courses had been rationalised to a certain extent, but there was still a significant overlap, which tended to cause friction. In addition, the status of University College had not been entirely clarified. The agreement between the two institutions was ambiguous in its wording: University College was said to be 'affiliated' with the University, but also 'to form part of it'. Was it an amalgamation of two equal partners, or was it

Above: The bombs which fell on the town on the night of 25 October 1940 inflicted significant damage on 'the Bute' and other buildings in the University's South Street complex. Hundreds of fragments of glass had to be removed from the bindings of library books.

[Photograph by George M Cowie; GMC-5-22-1]

Right: On the night of 5 August 1942 several bombs fell on Nelson Street in St Andrews, killing fourteen people.

[Photograph by George M Cowie; GMC-5-22-11]

an incorporation of the College within the University? By its founding statutes, University College had quite a different constitution from the University, another source of difficulty. There was dispute regarding whether St Andrews should be seen as the 'parent body': there had been, between 1883 and 1890, a strong body of opinion which sought the transferral of the University to Dundee. In an effort to overcome different approaches, the nineteenth-century negotiators had left a vagueness in the agreement which boded ill for the future. Throughout the 1890s a series of disputes, leading to litigation taken as far as the House of Lords, blighted the relationship between the two bodies, and in 1897 a new union was forged between them which did indeed incorporate University College within St Andrews University. The Dundee College's own College Council, under its founding statutes, remained in place, however, despite control of academic affairs now being vested in the University Senatus. Again, the ground for strife had been carefully prepared.

Despite the potential for conflict, the early years of the twentieth century did see significant development. New buildings for the Conjoint Medical School, a library, science and engineering department, and a teacher training college saw the establishment of the core of the Dundee campus before the outbreak of the First World War. In some areas, especially law, education and dental surgery, there was significant further growth in the inter-war years. Although Irvine seems sometimes to have had an ambivalent attitude to University College, he was certainly prepared to advance its interests as part of the overall institution. Notwithstanding, there remained a strong (and not entirely unjustified) feeling amongst staff in Dundee that the St Andrews establishment remained antagonistic to developments on the north side of the Tay; the conflict between the University Court and the College Council was fundamentally enshrined within in the constitutional set-up, and led to an ongoing atmosphere of friction.

Eventually, a royal commission led by Lord Tedder produced a report in 1952 recommending a formal overhaul of the institution's organisation. The result was legislation (the University of St Andrews Act, 1953) which finally ended the sixty-year-old ambiguity of the relationship between University Court and College Council by dissolving both governing bodies and forming a new University Court with full responsibility for the whole institution and properly representative of both parts of the University. Irvine did not live to see it implemented, however, dying in office in 1952. Within the new arrangement all the colleges were dissolved and re-formed, the Dundee college taking the new name of Queen's College. Whilst the following decade did see development, particularly in Dundee, with the institution of faculties of Law, Applied Sciences and Social Sciences, there remained dissatisfaction and resentment because of an apparent loss of traditional independence and control on both sides of the Tay.

During the 1950s Dundee grew faster than St Andrews, the latter being necessarily limited by the lack of expansion space within the historic town centre. The new Principal, Sir Malcolm Knox, previously Professor of Moral

The Museum of Zoology in University College, Dundee, founded by Professor D'Arcy Wentworth Thompson during his tenure of the chair of Biology (later Natural History) there from 1885 to 1917.

[Anon., c.1895–1900; ms42841/3]

Philosophy at St Andrews, had a hard act to follow. Although Irvine had been a controversial figure, he had presided over periods both of turmoil and of sustained growth, and he was well liked in St Andrews. One student of the 1930s describes him, even today, as a 'wonderful' man. Knox aimed to retain St Andrews as an elite, compact institution within the town centre with a limited student population, whilst encouraging the growth of the Dundee centre for the applied sciences and other 'professional' areas of study. Such a significant imbalance in student numbers, however, was not sustainable, and other, national, pressures to increase the size of the old University led to further development, from the mid-1960s, not within the town but on the North Haugh site on the western periphery. At the same time, the decision was made that two centres, potentially each of upwards of 3,000 students, could not continue as a single body, and that the long-term plan should therefore be to dissolve the union and establish Dundee as an independent institution.

The decision not to continue to pursue the model of a single university straddling the Tay cannot have been unrelated to developments on the national scene. Post-war Britain, in a period of unrivalled technological advance, was making demands which its education system was quite unable to meet. As had been the case during the innovative days of the industrial revolution more than a century earlier, the education system had to be modernised and expanded to fulfil the developing needs of modern society. In 1963 the report of a government committee tasked with examining the future of higher education throughout Britain – the 'Robbins Report' – recommended far-reaching changes, including a massive and rapid expansion of the system. New universities were to be created, many of them out of existing further education colleges, and a new breed of 'technological universities' was to be formed, primarily to satisfy industry's clamour for more graduates in the applied sciences. The result of

Sir Thomas Malcolm Knox,
Principal of the University
from 1953 to 1966.

[GPS]

the implementation of the Robbins plan for higher education was to double the number of universities in Scotland. Almost four centuries had passed since a new University had been founded north of the border, but four appeared in quick succession in the 1960s. Strathclyde University (1964) and Heriot-Watt University (1966) were formed respectively out of Glasgow's Anderson Institute and Edinburgh's Heriot-Watt College. Dundee came next, in 1967, with the envisaged split between Queen's College and St Andrews finally bringing to an end the experiment of extending the University of St Andrews to its industrial neighbour to the north, and providing the Dundee institution with the independent status which, by that stage, it required. Finally, in 1968 an entirely new University was formed on a greenfield site just outside Stirling. St Andrews now inhabited a new landscape in higher education.

Queen Elizabeth the Queen Mother meets students during her official visit to inaugurate the new University of Dundee in 1967.

[By kind permission of University of Dundee Archive Services; RPH-240-046]

8

A bullseye centred at the outer reaches

The student of the 1940s or 1950s was a member of a much larger and more mixed community than would have been found even half a century earlier. But still only a small minority of young people went to university, and the 2,000 or so students who lived in halls and in 'bunks' throughout St Andrews as the decade turned were a privileged few. The scrapbooks, journals and recollections of students in this period portray a life in which tradition and sociability played a major part. In the immediate post-war years, whilst continuing rationing sustained an atmosphere of wartime austerity, there was nonetheless hope: as ex-servicemen ('demobs') returned to the University, one female student commented that it was at last possible 'to find reasonable boyfriends', and hops and dances resumed as the core of the social scene. The traditional revelries of Raisin Monday (although it was banned for a time in the 1930s, when it became more rowdy than the University authorities could stomach) existed side-by-side with newer festivities such as the charities campaign with its accustomed public high-jinks. Rectorial elections, the

The students greet the new Rector, Lord Burghley, at the town's historic West Port, on 19 April 1950.

[Anon., from a photograph lent by C. B. Cowan; ms38585/1/C6/160]

Right: Traditionally, the new
Rector is 'dragged' through the
town by the students before his
installation. Here Sir Clement
Freud begins his drag in the
quadrangle, on 20 February 2003.

[Photograph by Peter Adamson;
PGA-E1665-40]

Below: On Sunday following the
service in St Salvator's chapel,
students go for a walk along the
harbour pier.

[Photograph by George M. Cowie,
c.1939; GMC-20-2-1]

annual Kate Kennedy procession, formal balls, tea parties, regular sports, frolics
on the sand and in the snow, Sunday morning walks on the pier, and vacation-
time foreign travels filled the students' lives along with the round of studies,
exams and ceremonies such as graduation. Although we think of it as a modern
phenomenon amongst the student community, the perpetration of alcohol-fuelled
pranks is not absent from student memories from the 1930s onwards!

Right: Each April, there is a
charity pageant organised by
the Kate Kennedy Club, in which
students parade through the town
dressed as significant characters
from the institution's and nation's
history. The eponymous Kate,
Lady Katherine Kennedy, was the
niece of Bishop James Kennedy,
the founder of St Salvator's
College. Her part is always played
by a first-year male student.
Shown here in 1938 are Kate,
the bishop, and the Rector of
the University, Lord Macgregor
Mitchell.

[Photograph by George M. Cowie;
GMC-18-81-19]

Below: A student 'bunk' in St
Andrews in the 1940s.

[Photograph: Anon., UYUYM]

Photographs show students in plain rooms in hall that were simply furnished and obviously cold, with small coal fires. Student reminiscences confirm these impressions: in the early 1960s a student in hall was provided with one bucket of coal for two days. They supplemented it with gathered driftwood, and shared each others' rooms in the evenings to save fuel. Because the rooms were cold, almost all study was done in the library. Halls were described as elegant, but shabby; after 1963 a fortunate few resided in the new Lumsden Wing of the all-female University Hall, with the luxury of underfloor heating. For women students particularly, life was still somewhat strictly disciplined: although hall life was 'convivial', the female student of the early 1960s was seriously told by the senior warden – as were those of the 1930s – that men's 'baser instincts' became largely uncontrollable after 10.00 p.m., and that they should therefore return to their rooms by that hour. No male visitors were allowed in hall rooms unless in the presence of other females. Nonetheless, the memories are happy, infused both with collegiality and with the historic atmosphere of the medieval town and university. The teaching was reckoned to be of a high standard, and took place both in college and, echoing much earlier practice, in the private homes of the staff, some of whom also held regular tea or sherry parties for their students.

One theme which is common to the memories of many students from the central years of the twentieth century is the towering presence of Sir D'Arcy Wentworth Thompson. When he died in 1948, Principal Irvine's tribute to him in the University magazine, *College Echoes*, stated that 'never again in the academic history of this country is it conceivable that a University will be confronted with the pious duty of paying tribute to a Professor who occupied his Chair for an unbroken period of no less than sixty-four years'. Born in 1860, he was appointed Professor of Biology in University College Dundee in 1885, when still in his mid-twenties. A much-admired teacher, he was also a prolific researcher and author, his most important work being *On Growth and Form*, a study of the mathematical

Professor D'Arcy Wentworth Thompson as a young man in 1886, and later in life, c.1943.

[Photograph by Robertson, Dundee; ms50128/2; anon.; ms50125/1]

basis of the nature of growth in the natural world. It was published in 1917 (and subsequently in several editions, and in many languages), and has become a classic pioneering text, still in print today. Also in 1917 he moved to the Chair of Natural History in St Andrews, a post which he was to hold – still actively teaching – until his death over thirty years later. A noted polymath, he translated Aristotle from the Greek, and could teach fluently on mathematics, classics and physics as well as in his home territory of biology or natural history. At Dundee and in St Andrews he developed natural history museums, the collections of which remain, both as public and academic resources. With a personality and physical presence as impressive as his intellect, his influence on every aspect of the University's life must be as great as almost any other individual figure in its history.

Although revered, D'Arcy Thompson was certainly not the only eminent academic in the University. From 1888 to 1919 the chair of Botany in University College, Dundee was held by Patrick Geddes, best known today as an early pioneer of town planning. Within D'Arcy Thompson's lifetime the University welcomed its very first female professor, and indeed the first in any Scottish university. A pioneer of the use of radium in Scotland in the treatment of cancers, following the work of Marie Curie, Margaret Fairlie was appointed to the Chair

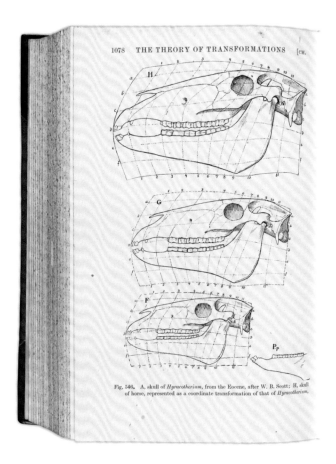

One of the 'transformation' diagrams from D'Arcy Wentworth Thompson's *On Growth and Form*, demonstrating how variations in the physical form of related species can be mathematically modelled. The photograph is taken from D.W.T.'s own, heavily annotated, copy of the second (1942) edition.

[ms42363/4]

of Obstetrics and Gynaecology in 1940. (The progressive attitude to gender was not maintained, however. It was more than half a century before Ursula Martin became the second female professor in the University, appointed to the Chair of Computational Science in 1992.) Throughout the 1950s the John Napier Chair of Astronomy was held by Erwin Findlay Freundlich, an associate of Einstein and Eddington who had previously taught in both Istanbul and Prague. In 1945 the University's new Master of Music was Cedric Thorpe Davie, a Scottish-born composer who had studied with Kodály. Rising eventually to become Professor of Music in 1973, he almost single-handedly built the Department of Music, and largely created the institution's reputation as 'the singing university'. His eminence as a Scottish composer greatly enhanced the University's musical reputation.

Much of the routine lives of students continued to revolve around the many societies, which had begun to make their appearance as early as the mid-eighteenth century. The earliest society of which records survive is the Theological Society, which came into being in the 1760s, followed towards the end of the century by the Celtic Society, the early records of which provide a rare example of written Perthshire Gaelic. Throughout the nineteenth century a plethora of sporting, subject-based and religious societies sprang up, a trend which has continued into modern times. Curiously, in 1924 there was an attempt by the University to abolish all existing societies, and to replace them with one literary and one scientific society. The irrepressible curiosity and conviviality of the student body made short work of the bid to exert such authoritarian control over their social activities, however, and the number and range continued to grow. Today, any group which meets the Student Association's criteria (fundamentally that it has twenty or more matriculated student members, and has a constitution

Below left: Scotland's first female university professor, Margaret Fairlie.

[Photograph: Anon.; GPS]

Below right: Erwin Findlay Freundlich, Professor of Astronomy and associate of Einstein and Eddington.

[Photograph: Anon.; GPS]

approved by the Association) can become affiliated, and is thus part of the Students' Association, eligible to receive grants and other support from it. Over 120 societies jostle for members at the annual Freshers' Fair: they are sporting, dramatic, musical, debating, political, religious, academic, charitable and the purely social, encompassing as diverse a range as A Capella, Business Ethics, Dr Who, Fine Chocolate, Gilbert and Sullivan, Knitting, Neuroscience, Photography, Real Ale, Swing Dance, Tunnocks Caramel Wafer Appreciation, Wargaming, and many, many more. The activities of societies offer opportunities beyond the social and academic, too: St Andrews' 'Sports Hall of Fame' includes several Olympians (including the current Chancellor, Sir Menzies Campbell), and many internationalists and award winners in a range of team and individual sports. Students, through their societies, also regularly raise annual sums well into six figures for a variety of local, national and international charities.

One student, although overwhelmingly positive about her undergraduate experience in St Andrews in the late 1930s, nonetheless described it as a very class-conscious place, where snobbishness abounded. Today's town and University are much less so, she thought. This is a reputation from which St Andrews has suffered for many years. Partly based on an inaccurate impression that it is an 'English-style', collegiate university, it has been dubbed a haven for the privately educated, upper-class student from south of the border. But statistics do not support the stereotype. Like any other institution with a fine academic reputation, St Andrews attracts a wide range of students, from a broad diversity

One of St Andrews' more curious student societies is The Tunnock's Caramel Wafer Appreciation Society, which was started in 1982, primarily to raise money for charity.

[Photograph by Peter Adamson, 1999; PGA7-51]

of backgrounds. At the end of the 1940s, of the total (c. 2,200) student population of the University, over 65 per cent gave home addresses in Scotland; less than 30 per cent gave home addresses in England, and only a little over 5 per cent came from other parts of the UK or overseas. Around 60 per cent of all students were educated in state schools. It is true that these figures were influenced by the presence of the Conjoint Medical School in Dundee, and the fact that many applied subjects were taught on the Dundee campus, which attracted a large majority of Scottish-based students. Even removing the students with term-time residence in Dundee, however, it is clear that the student population of St Andrews itself was almost 60 per cent Scottish, less than 35 per cent English, and a little over 5 per cent from elsewhere. Well under half of the students studying in St Andrews itself had private-school backgrounds. Given the difficulty of funding a university education in days prior to (and, indeed, subsequent to) universal student grants, a sizeable proportion of privately educated students is to be expected, and does not differ significantly from other comparable institutions. Following the establishment of the University of Dundee, the balance shifted a little: in the early 1980s, out of a total student population of a little over 3,500, just over 50 per cent came from elsewhere in the UK, about 6 per cent from overseas locations, and the remainder – still over 40 per cent – from Scottish homes. (The breakdown of school backgrounds is not known for that period.) Still, the numbers do not bear out the popular image of a University massively dominated by one group or another.

One of a series of cartoons, mimicking contemporary commercial advertisements, which promoted various aspects of University life: in this instance, the Chemistry Society.

[c.1945–7, from an original lent by C.B. Cowan; ms38585/2/1]

EACH OCTOBER THE STUDENT BODY SCOURS THE TOWN FOR BUNKS; BUT THE LUCKY FEW.......

THEY'RE OFF TO JOIN THE CHEM. SOC.!

Today's students continue to revel in tradition and sociability, but they are part of a yet larger community, now comprising a staff and student body amounting to 9,000 individuals. The facilities available to them have expanded and improved immeasurably, due partly to the policy of successive governments to extend the opportunity for higher education to an ever-larger proportion of the community, and partly to the massive social and economic changes of the later twentieth century, which created an international educational marketplace in which universities worldwide compete for funds, reputation and students. Today, although in no sense a 'private' university, St Andrews receives less than 20 per cent of its core funding directly from government. The rest comes from a dazzling array of research funding awards, from sponsored research, from spin-off companies, from fees, and from funds provided by generous individual benefactors, including alumni.

The changing nature of University funding has made the recruitment of overseas students ever more important to the financial security of universities, and the demographic picture has altered radically. The overall student population in St Andrews has more than doubled since the 1980s and now rests at around 7,500. Equally remarkably, though, the split between country of domicile now gives around 30 per cent each from Scotland and England (with the rest of

The St Salvator's quadrangle fills with students as lectures change.

the UK still a tiny proportion), about 30 per cent from the European Union, and a further 10 per cent from other overseas locations. Still, as in the 1940s, a little over 60 per cent of the entrants under the age of twenty-one come from the state school sector. This huge increase in the number of overseas students means that today's student experience is far more culturally diverse and cosmopolitan than has previously been the case. Indeed, it seems that in some respects the modern 'global market' in higher education is reminiscent of the medieval practice by which scholars travelled Europe, largely without attention to boundaries, in search of learning at the feet of scholars of international reputation. It is undoubtedly the case that as straightforward 'block grant' funding from central government has declined as a proportion of universities' income, the fees paid by overseas students have become a crucial element of the University's financial viability. Effective marketing, and the drive to maintain a word-class reputation for teaching and research across many disciplines is therefore vital to survival in an increasingly competitive marketplace.

A glance at the Students' Association website emphasises the importance which both the University's management and the student body itself place on the involvement of students in the running of the institution. Students elect those who will run the Students' Association and those who will represent their interests to the University. Student representatives sit on most of the major University committees, and their interests are further represented by the Rector, who is elected by them every three years. It has not always been so. Until relatively recently the student body was subject to a much more authoritarian regime, in which disagreement with official policy had no formal voice and thus often took the form only of public protest, which frequently led to disciplinary action. Things began to change in the later nineteenth century, however, with the foundation in 1885 of the Students' Representative Council (SRC). In 1889 its existence was formally recognised in the Universities (Scotland) Act, and a University Ordinance in 1895 defined its functions within the University. It existed to represent the interests of the students, to offer a means by which communication between the students and the University could be improved, and to promote social life and collegiality amongst the students. In 1889 it founded a student magazine, *College Echoes*, the first of many student publications which have persisted to the present day. A Students' Union (for men only, of course) was founded in 1888 and, in 1904, with financial support from Mrs Andrew Carnegie, a women's Union was eventually founded. The two Unions amalgamated to form one Students' Union in 1963. As early as the 1940s, however, there was some unrest in St Andrews, as in many universities throughout the UK and Europe, since the student populations felt, not unreasonably, that their concerns and ideas were not adequately represented or heard. Annual International Student Congresses repeatedly voiced such concerns, and as the post-war years gave way to the more open and questioning society of the 1960s, the calls became louder and clearer.

The Old Union building on North Street, the site of the first Student's Union, founded in 1886.

Although the formal structures of student representation did not change in St Andrews until later, the changing society of the 1960s was evident in other ways. The traditional 'hops' and formal dances which had characterised social life in the 1940s and 1950s began to give way to a broader diet of popular events, including, of course, concerts by the pop groups of the day. St Andrews was small, however, and events seem to have been limited in scale. There was some – but minimal – collaboration between the student bodies of Dundee and St Andrews universities after 1966, but when an event of a large scale was planned early in 1969 it was controversial. A letter from the Union's Entertainments Convenor in the pages of *Aien*, the then student newspaper, claimed that if the planned concert was a success it would 'be seen as a take-off point, and the alternatives open to the next Entertainments Convenor are endless. If, however, the concert loses a lot of money, St Andrews, as far as Entertainments is concerned, must slip back into inglorious isolation . . . the Union will have to fall back . . . on a diet of obscure bands.' The event in question was none other than a visit of 'the biggest name and least Establishment band that has ever come to St Andrews' – Pink Floyd, who raised the rafters in the rather staid surroundings of the Younger Hall on the night of 16 February 1969.

Musically, it seems to have been a success (although no formal review of the concert appears to have been written), but despite the controversy about the financial advisability of trying to bring such a major act to the town, marketing and publicity had been poor – the Dundee student body, for example, seems not to have known of it – and the concert did indeed lose money. Although 520 people turned up, the Union lost £70 on the event; this was a significant sum in 1969.

Top: An article in the student newspaper, *Aien*, discussing the anticipated Pink Floyd concert, which was held in the Younger Hall in 1969.

Below left: A ticket for the 1949 Charities Ball, one of the more formal of such functions which are held throughout the academic year.

[ms38462]

Below right: The current student union building in St Mary's Place, opened in 1973, is home to the Students' Association, and a venue for many student activities.

The Pink Floyd

The Pink Floyd, the biggest name and least Establishment band that has ever come to St Andrews. At a cost of £350, the group has been hired for a Sunday evening concert NEXT Sunday evening, in the Younger Hall, which also hosts the Corries this week. The success of the Pink Floyd concert is crucial for both the Union and St Andrews students in toto: the Union are investing a large amount of money in the venture—if it is a success then the Floyd establish the fact that there are enough students here willing to pay to listen to national groups. Peter West, the Union Entertainment Convener, explains the nature of this breakthrough on page two of this edition of AIEN. The situation so far looks promising: in the first few days of sales, over 100 Hounam-designed tickets, at 10/- per head, were sold from the Union Committee Room. But the Union must fill the Younger to capacity—around 800—to break even on the concert, which will also feature a Glasgow band supporting the Floyd. The Pink Floyd means the future of St Andrews popular music—if they are a success, then more groups of such standing can be lured to St Andrews—witness Elmer Gantry's Velvet Opera already hired for a Charities Week gig.

It was not the financial disaster that had been predicted by some, however, and the Union survived to put on other mainstream acts in following years, such as the hugely popular Hawkwind, in 1971. In 1973 a new Union building was opened, offering a huge improvement in facilities, including bars and event venues. The need to improve and reorganise student representation in the University was eventually recognised in 1983, with the foundation of the Students' Association in its present form, at which point the Union and the SRC were restructured to form constituent parts of the Association.

The increasing role of the Students' Association in the University, and the parallel prominence of student newspapers, gave opportunity for some to use their student days as a proving ground for future political careers. For example, the present First Minister of Scotland, Alex Salmond, graduated with an MA in Economics and History in 1978, and he was a student contemporary of a political opponent, former Secretary of State for Scotland, Michael Forsyth.

A young Alex Salmond (far left) with the Scottish Nationalist MP Winnie Ewing (centre, front) on her visit to St Andrews in October 1977.

[Photograph by George M. Cowie; GMC-FI306-6]

If the nature of the student body and its lifestyle have developed rapidly in the post-war years, so has the physical presence of the University within the town. The Universities (Scotland) Act of 1966 had reorganised the University, making changes to collegiate structure and to the composition of Court and Senate, but it did little to offer the University a new direction in the challenging, post-Dundee era. Principal Knox resigned when the arrangements for the split with Dundee had been made; he was succeeded by John Steven Watson, an eminent historian who had no previous connection with St Andrews, a fact which was perhaps to his advantage, as he had no association with either party in the divisive situation which preceded his appointment. It seemed clear that in an age when Universities were growing both in size and number, St Andrews needed to develop well beyond its diminished presence if it was to flourish once more. Rapid expansion took place. Within very few years the student body had increased by some 50 per cent, and an extraordinarily ambitious building programme was under way.

The roots of this development went further back, however: even in the 1950s it had been clear that the town-centre accommodation for academic departments as well as, for instance, the University Library, were seriously inadequate. Well endowed with the charm of the medieval townscape, they lacked the space and the facilities required by a modern university. Principal Knox had firmly pursued a policy of maintaining the development of the University in a compact form within the historic town centre. A site to the east of the St Mary's College and Bute Buildings complex on South Street was identified for development. As it was in private hands, and the proposal for large-scale development within the town centre was consistently controversial, the site proved in the long run impractical. The North Haugh, on the western periphery of the town, was instead adopted when, in 1960, it was made available for purchase. On this site the urgent need for scientific teaching and laboratory space was to be met from 1964 onwards, as the relocation of the departments of Physics, Mathematics and Chemistry from the town centre enabled the gradual expansion of arts subjects into the spaces thus vacated. The North Haugh has continued to be developed, primarily as a 'science campus', now housing also Computer Science, Biological Sciences, and the schools of both Medicine and Management, as well as a high proportion of the University's residences.

Town-centre expansion also continued: the Students' Union on St Mary's Place was the first of the major developments, followed in 1974 by the new Buchanan Building, primarily for the Department of Modern Languages, on Union Street. A new University Library opened on North Street in 1976, and a variety of residential and other developments (such as a new Sports Centre) accompanied these, in both central and peripheral locations. The purchase of additional town-centre properties also enabled expansion of the traditional disciplines. The 1970s, then, saw development of the University, and thus changes to the nature

The North Haugh, on the western periphery of the town, has been developing, primarily as a science and residential campus, since the 1960s.

of the town, on an unprecedented scale. As student numbers increased, so did the requirement for both academic and support staff. Partly fuelled by the call for housing to meet the needs of the expanding University, St Andrews itself grew, with large-scale residential development taking place, particularly to the south. By the end of the 1970s the University and town had changed radically in both character and physical appearance.

In the early 1980s, changes in government policy, with an ideological aversion to far-reaching social expenditure by government, caused retrenchment. Further expansion of UK student numbers was discouraged; universal student grants were phased out; staff numbers throughout the university sector were to be reduced in line with general budgetary cuts; and even some departments were to be amalgamated, or closed altogether. The expansion of St Andrews University in the previous decade had been so profound that it was able to weather the storm relatively intact, although the departments of Linguistics, Archaeology and (a little later) Music were lost. Their loss was a severe blow. Coming so soon after the retirement of Cedric Thorpe Davie in 1978, it is perhaps a remarkable testament to the strength of the school he had built that music continued to thrive. Some teaching continues within the University, and through the University's Music Centre and many societies, musical activity in the University remains vibrant. In recent years, too, the University has validated the postgraduate degrees of the Royal Scottish Academy of Music and Drama. It is also now the first university in Scotland to have a professional orchestra in residence, through its close association with the Scottish Chamber Orchestra.

The financial realities of this period, however, also prompted the universities into the drive towards recruiting additional overseas students. Steven Watson

Right: The new University Library under construction. Opened in 1976, it was intended to be the first of three phases of construction, but the subsequent phases were not undertaken. An extensive refurbishment of the building is planned for 2011/12.

[StAU-NorS-Lib-109]

Opposite: Music-making, with its home in the Younger Hall, has for long been central to University life in St Andrews.

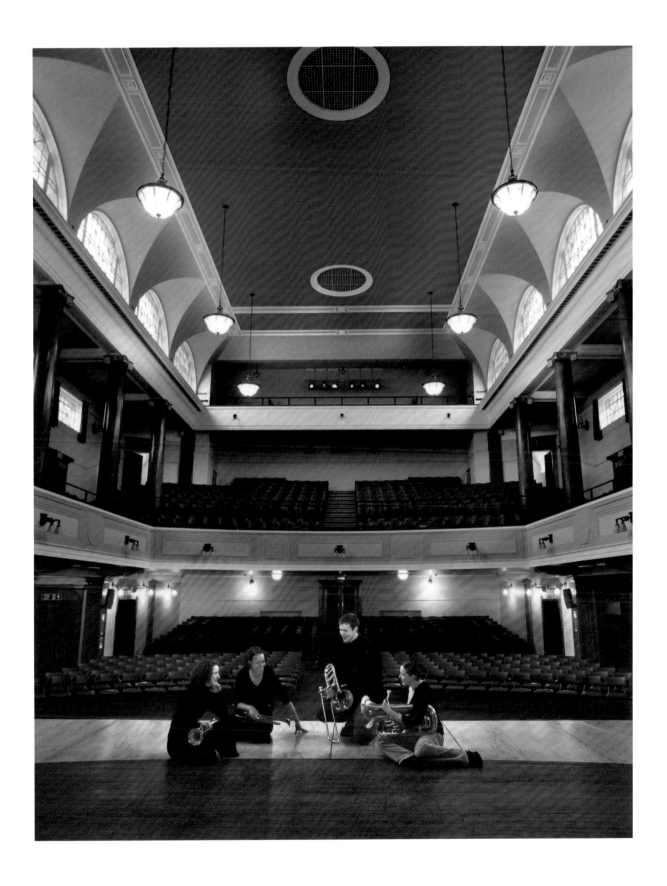

retired in 1986; sadly, he died only a matter of weeks thereafter. He left St Andrews planning for a future in which it would extend its reputation internationally, not just as a university with a long and distinctive tradition behind it, but one with a forward-looking approach, high academic standards, and offering a place where both scholars and staff benefited from a unique lifestyle. Watson's successor as Principal, scientist Struther Arnott, recognised the increasing importance of building a research profile appropriate for a modern, competitive educational environment. He largely restructured the University, and pursued an aggressive policy towards recruitment of high-reputation staff with active research profiles. Often a controversial figure within the University, his policies may well be applauded by later historians, since, although undoubtedly causing short-term financial difficulties, they were probably in the longer term responsible for the exalted research and teaching reputation which the institution has developed. Arnott's successor from 2001 until 2008, Brian Lang, came to the University having been previously the chief executive of the British Library. Building on and extending the work done by Arnott, Lang continued to build the brand of St Andrews, and attempted further to streamline its governance, moving it some way towards being a 'managed' rather than an 'administered' institution, and tried both to develop its fundraising potential and to enhance its international reputation.

The nature of the educational experience has changed every bit as much as the students' lifestyle and the physical nature of the town and University. The greatest change has come about with the advent of computers. Although the potential of computing within the University had been under discussion since the 1950s (and some tentative steps had already been taken in Queen's

Brian Lang, Principal of the University from 2001 to 2008, leaves a graduation ceremony with the Chancellor, Sir Menzies Campbell.

College, Dundee), the first computer in St Andrews was installed in late 1964 at the University Observatory's Scott Lang building, largely through the efforts of Professor Walter Stibbs, the Professor of Astronomy. An IBM 1620 Model II machine, it came at the discounted but nonetheless colossal cost of £60,000. A computing service for the University soon followed, but in those early days none can have seriously entertained the notion that the computer would soon have such a ubiquitous presence in our lives. Initially of benefit primarily for the computational requirements of the scientific community, the electronic revolution has subsequently spread to every aspect of life and pervades all disciplines within the University, affecting both the availability of information and the nature of study, research and teaching. In an era where the online pedagogical presence can be as important as personal contact; where the majority of students carry their own computers with them to classes and tutorials; where the presence of extensive computing facilities and the delivery of online literature is a core requirement of a library; where the overwhelming majority of administrative and personal correspondence is carried out by email; and where the internet tool is becoming a basic function of even a mobile telephone, the world of the University is indeed transformed.

Information technology is also an important factor in the internationalisation of education. The ease of communication as well as of travel greatly facilitates the presence of overseas students and staff in the University but, perhaps more importantly, the collaboration with far-flung individuals, teams and institutions massively enhances the opportunities for research and teaching to international standards. As in the medieval university, higher education in the modern age is an international enterprise.

The first computer in St Andrews, installed in 1964.

[Photograph reproduced by kind permission of Dr T.R. Carson]

The ubiquitous computer: information technology is now central to study in every discipline.

Staff come to St Andrews from many parts of the world, and research projects in science and the arts include collaborations and funding bodies across many international borders. The St Andrews Prize for the Environment annually attracts entries offering innovative solutions to environmental problems from around fifty countries. No fewer than twenty-four St Andrews Alumni clubs meet in cities spanning ten different countries on five continents. Year on year, the pages of the newspapers and of alumni and staff magazines are filled with reports of ground-breaking research in every field of endeavour – the environment, medicine, pure and applied sciences, society and the humanities – funded from government and private sources from across the globe. The internationalism of the modern University is perhaps emphasised most strongly by the appointment as Principal, in succession to Brian Lang, of Professor Louise Richardson, the University's first female Principal, who assumed the position in January 2009. Professor Richardson is a scholar who is international in more than one sense. Growing up and studying first in the Republic of Ireland, she then undertook postgraduate study at Harvard University in Boston, and came to St Andrews having previously served as Executive Dean of the Radcliffe Institute for Advanced Study at Harvard. Equally telling is that her own academic special-ism is in the discipline of International Relations, an important area of growth for St Andrews, which inaugurated its Centre for the Study of Terrorism and Political Violence in 1994, the first such body in Europe.

In this environment, reputation is critical. Honours and awards to the institution, its institutes and its staff abound. Equally, however, the University has to be proud of those whom it chooses to honour. In the last couple of decades, honorary degrees have been bestowed upon those at the very top of their respective fields. These have included: from the arts, musician Bob Dylan, actress Joanna Lumley and writers Kazuo Ishiguro, Fay Weldon and Douglas Dunn; from the world of business, Sir Tom Farmer; from the world of politics, Sir David Steel; from the world of sport, Sir Chris Hoy, Sir Alex Ferguson and golfers Severiano Ballesteros, Colin Montgomerie and Arnold Palmer; from the media, John Simpson and Sir Trevor McDonald; from the world of religion, the Dalai Lama and Cardinal Archbishop Keith O'Brien; and many, many eminent academics from every field of study. Rightly, the University also honours its own. The geographer Dr Kathleen McIver, for instance, received the degree of LLD in 1991 in recognition of her outstanding contribution to the University. She had successively been its first female Departmental Chair, its first female Dean of Arts, and its first female Master of the United College. David Corner, Lecturer in Medieval History, later Secretary and Registrar, and finally Deputy Principal of the University, was honoured on his retirement in 2006 from more than thirty years of service, for his 'massive contribution to the health, well-being and success of the University'. The University's honorary graduates are in themselves a measure of its continuing distinction.

Results from official measures of success, such as the government's Research Assessment Exercise, bolster the claim of excellence. In 2008, for instance, 94 per cent of St Andrews' research activity was deemed internationally recognised, and 60 per cent was reckoned to be world leading or internationally excellent. Regularly ranking amongst the top universities in both Scotland and the UK, St Andrews is consistently placed amongst the best in Scotland, and within the top five or ten British universities in a range of surveys. Its claim to be 'one of the leading research-intensive universities in the world' is neither idle rhetoric nor coincidence: it is deliberate policy, as demonstrated by the University's mission statement, enshrined within its strategic plan, 'to achieve the highest international standards of excellence in scholarship, manifested in the quality of its research and of its graduates'. As the first decade of the twenty-first century

Professor Louise Richardson is congratulated by the Chancellor on her installation as Principal on 25 March 2009.

came to a close, a UK-wide student survey voted St Andrews first-equal in terms of the students' own satisfaction with the quality of their higher educational experience, the fifth successive year that the University topped the poll.

League tables are necessarily both partial and controversial, but they are symptomatic of the effort which has to be applied to create the reputation and the distinctive 'brand' which will enable a small institution to survive in such a competitive environment. As this book goes to press, the UK, in common with much of the world, is struggling with economic challenge, and severe cutbacks in public spending hang over the higher education sector. If it is to retain its market share, the University, as periodically throughout its history, has to be creatively determined in pursuing high-calibre students and staff, and in maintaining the highest reputation of excellence: in effect, to 'grow the business'. An ambitious building programme is again under way, to provide new, state-of-the-art facilities. Press releases record continuing high-profile appointments. Dynamic plans for the 600th anniversary, with its accompanying appeal, demonstrate that, irrespective of temporary economic circumstances, the University looks forward to a seventh century of expansion and improvement.

We began this survey of the University by asking 'why St Andrews?' The University's staff magazine, *The St Andard*, carries a regular feature that quizzes members of the academic staff on what attracts them to St Andrews, and what makes them stay. The answers are remarkably consistent across disciplines as

Quality of education, community and, of course, tradition, all play their part in the outstanding St Andrews student experience.

[Photograph reproduced by kind permission of Ben Goulter]

diverse as Medieval History and Solar Physics: the initial attractions are most often the strength of the discipline and of the academic team they will be joining, and the environment in which they will live and study. They stay because of a supportive and active research community and for the atmosphere of the local and national surroundings – 'a great place to live and work'; 'why ever would one leave?' The natural and the academic environments combine with a realistic sense of its history to make this small town a place which still attracts thousands of people to live and study. St Andrews has become less remote as the centuries have passed – the world contains fewer and fewer truly remote places – but it still cannot claim to be geographically central. Throughout its history scholars have crossed lands and oceans to study here.

In the constant upheaval of change we treasure solid and visible links to the past: relics of ecclesiastic splendour, of siege and battle clinging now to cliff-edge. In a world instantly at our fingertips we value the open sky, expanse of sea and swathe of green. Six hundred years old, aware of its past, but facing forward, St Andrews remains distinct. The bullseye is not simply a tiny point for which to aim; it also represents high reward. Now, more than ever throughout its long, sometimes troubled and often distinguished history, the University of St Andrews invites the highest objective: 'ever to excel'.

A bullseye centred at the outer reaches.

Notes on sources

These notes do not constitute a bibliography for the work. They offer guidance to some of the main archival sources for the history of the University, and some suggestions for further background reading. A general statement is followed by brief comments specific to each chapter.

The University's archives

The institutional archives of the University of St Andrews, known as its Muniments, are impressive. Occupying about one linear kilometre of shelves, they hold a wealth of material relating to the administration, landholding, and academic affairs of the institution, its staff and students. It would be inappropriate here to give a comprehensive guide to the records available, but some of the series of records most heavily used are briefly described below. The wider archival resources of the University, also held in the University Library's Special Collections Department, include manuscript collections which have been acquired by gift and purchase over many years. These include significant amounts of record material relating to former staff and students of the University. The rare book collections (which include many volumes which have been owned by the University for centuries, as well as the bequeathed libraries of former staff), and the extensive photographic collections are also a rich source of information. Currently the best published guide to the Muniments is available from the Archives Hub website, at http://www.archiveshub.ac.uk. A developing in-house online catalogue also provides very detailed information on both muniment and more general manuscript collections, available from www://st-andrews.ac.ukspecialcollections. The library's online book catalogue is 'SAULCAT'. For further information regarding the photographic holdings, see the note to Chapter 6, below.

Much of the material describing the institution's early days is taken from the magnificent records of the Faculty of Arts, the first minute book of which covers the period 1413–1728. After 1588 it is largely restricted to records of the election of University officials, but prior to that date it describes in sometimes minute detail the day-to-day working of the University. The archival reference for the original volume is UYUY411/1. The part of it covering the period to 1588 is also available in print, in a fine edition, with a detailed introductory analysis which is still the best available description of the early university: *Acta Facultatis Artium Universitatis Sanctiandree, 1413–1588*, edited by A.I. Dunlop (Edinburgh & London, 1964). The series continues in separate volumes (with some gaps) to 1954 (UYUY411/4–9). The record continues to the present day within several different series.

The matriculation and graduation records of the University from 1470 onwards comprise several series of records within the classification UYUY300. Much of the information quoted regarding the attendance of specific students comes from the remarkable single volume which records the matriculation and graduation of students between 1536 and 1859 (UYUY305/2), although supplementary information is frequently to be found also in the financial records, such as the Faculty of Arts Bursar's Book, 1456–1853 (UYUY412), and the Faculty of Arts minutes books described above.

Collations of parts of these records, providing a useful index to students whose names appear in the records, was undertaken in two publications by James Maitland Anderson, *Early Records of the University of St Andrews* (Scottish History Society: Edinburgh, 1926) and *The Matriculation Roll of the University of St Andrews, 1747–1897* (Edinburgh, 1905). These have more recently been supplemented by R.N. Smart's magisterial *Biographical Register of the University of St Andrews, 1747–1897* (St Andrews, 2004) and his subsequent *Biographical Register of the University of St Andrews, 1579–1747* (due for publication in 2011), which briefly detail what is known of the careers of all members of the University in those periods.

From 1696, a major source of information is the ongoing series of minute books of the University Senatus. This record details the academic affairs of the University, including the granting of medical and honorary degrees, up to the present day (UYUY452). In very modern times the Senatus has been augmented by an executive Academic Council.

Similarly, the minute books of St Leonard's College (UYSL400), St Mary's College (UYSM400) and United College (UYUC400) provide an account, often detailed, of their activities throughout their independent histories. The colleges, too, all have extensive series of 'Inventoried Papers' (UYSS110, UYSL110, UYSM110, UYUC110), which contain tenurial and other records relating to the administration of their affairs from medieval times into the nineteenth century.

Regular mention is made throughout the text to the extensive series of commissions and 'visitations' which so deeply influenced the development of the University throughout its history. The records of these are scattered, and defy any real attempt to describe them comprehensively in a limited space. Working papers of some survive within the National Archives of Scotland (see http://www.nas.gov.uk); others are represented within the 'Inventoried Papers' series of the college archives (see above) and in a small collection within the non-collegiate University records at UYUY812. The published records – including submissions by, and interviews of, the staff of the University – of the major nineteenth-century commissions also provide a delightfully detailed account of the University in the respective periods, and preserve the texts of many of the key constitutional documents. These include some (such as the five missing papal founding bulls) which are no longer extant in the original but were printed for the commissioners from earlier transcripts. See J.H. Baxter's *Bibliography*, noted under 'Secondary Reading', below, for details of these publications.

The University *Calendars*, published from 1852 until superseded by web-accessible information in 2002, provide a wealth of information about staff and courses, and are an invaluable source of statistical information. The cessation of publication of this broad-ranging information in one easily referenced source is much to be lamented. More detailed statistical analysis (as offered in Chapter 8) has been undertaken generally from individual student matriculation records, which are not publicly accessible. The most modern statistics have been obtained from the University's electronic admissions records.

The records of the modern Principals and some other key functionaries within the University are also an important source. The official papers of most twentieth century Principals are preserved in the archives at UYUY250, some more voluminous than others. Some earlier Principals, notably James David Forbes (Principal of United College from 1859 to 1868) and Sir James Donaldson (Principal of United College, 1886–96 and then of the University, 1896–1915) are well represented by collections of mixed official and personal papers held within the University Library's manuscript collections. For details of these and the papers of other important individuals (such as Sir D'Arcy Wentworth Thompson), refer to: http://www.standrews.ac.uk/specialcollections.

At several points throughout the text mention is made of the records of the University Library. Part of the Muniment collections, the library records provide a fine portrayal of the development of the library, both centrally and within the colleges, primarily from the late seventeenth century onwards. Of particular relevance are the catalogues of holdings (from 1695 to date, with some earlier fragmentary records) and the library's borrowing registers, which, in several series relating to the borrowings of both students and professors, record the use of the library from the end of the seventeenth century until the implementation of an electronic circulation system in 1976. The overall series reference for the library records is UYLY, and a full listing of the records is available in the online Manuscript and Muniment catalogue.

Secondary reading

The history of the University itself has not yet been comprehensively written. Some articles of interest to specific periods and episodes are noted below under each chapter. The only previous historical survey of the institution is R.G. Cant, *A Short History of the University of St Andrews* (4th edition, St Andrews, 2002). A set of historical essays was part of a range of publications in connection with the University's quincentenary celebrations in 1911, and published under the title *Votiva Tabella* (St Andrews, 1911).

Brief histories of the colleges of St Salvator and St Leonard have been published: Ronald G. Cant, *The College of St Salvator* (Edinburgh, 1950) and John Herkless and Robert Kerr Hannay, *The College of St Leonard* (Edinburgh, 1905), and much useful background is also provided in Annie I. Dunlop, *The Life and Times of James Kennedy, Bishop of St Andrews* (Edinburgh, 1950). For St Salvator's, see also R.G. Cant, *St Salvator's Chapel, St Andrews: The College and Collegiate Kirk of St Salvator: A Short Account of the Building and its History* (St Andrews, 1971); and *Veterum Laudes, Being a Tribute to the Achievements of the Members of St Salvator's College during Five Hundred Years*, ed. J.B. Salmond (Edinburgh, 1950). For St Leonard's, see also R.G. Cant, *St Leonard's Chapel: The Kirk and College of St Leonard: A Short Account of the Building and its History* (St Andrews, 1970). For St Mary's College, see D.W.D. Shaw, *In Divers Manners: A St Mary's Miscellany: To Commemorate the 450th Anniversary of St Mary's College, 7 March, 1539* (St Andrews, 1990); and J.K. Cameron, 'A Trilingual College for Scotland: The Founding of St Mary's College', in *St Mary's Bulletin*, 1989, pp. 9–19.

J.G.S. Blair, *A History of Medicine in the University of St Andrews* (Edinburgh, 1987) provides a wide chronological coverage and much contextual information.

The history of civic St Andrews is poorly served. Snapshots of the town can be obtained from well-known sources such as the first (1791) and second (1855) *Statistical Accounts*. The town is also well covered in the nineteenth-century local historical works such as A.H. Millar's *Fife Pictorial and Historical: Its People, Burghs, Castles, and Mansions* (Cupar, 1895), Walter Wood's *The East Neuk of Fife: Its History and Antiquities* (2nd edition, Edinburgh 1887), and in many tourist-oriented guides from the early nineteenth century onwards.

Rev. Charles Lyon's *History of St Andrews, Episcopal, Monastic, Academic and Civil* (2 volumes, Edinburgh, 1843) is heavily ecclesiastical in its outlook, but is also in parts engagingly detailed. Most modern work has tended to be pictorial in nature, or to concentrate on specific areas, such as the history of golf or family history. Many useful articles on specific issues have been published in the *Yearbooks* (from 1959) of the St Andrews Preservation Trust. Extensive information regarding writings about St Andrews prior to 1926 is to be found in J.H. Baxter, *Collections Towards a Bibliography of St Andrews* (St Andrews, 1926).

The contextual history of Scotland, England, Britain and Europe are well served by many single and multi-volume works of great distinction. Particularly useful for the general background history of Scotland is *The Edinburgh History of Scotland* (4 volumes, Edinburgh, 1987–1989). There are many more detailed treatments of specific periods and aspects of Scotland's history.

The best source of information regarding the medieval universities of Europe remains H. Rashdall, *The Universities of Europe in the Middle Ages*, ed. F.M. Powicke and A.B. Emden (3 volumes, Oxford, 1936).

The source for all Scottish parliamentary proceedings is the ground-breaking, searchable web-based edition of the Records of the Parliaments of Scotland, produced by a research team based in St Andrews, available at http://www.rps.ac.uk.

Chapter 1

Bower's description of the foundation of the University (and of the celebrations detailed in Chapter 2) come from the modern edition, in the original Latin with a parallel translation – produced over more than a decade under the editorship of Professor Donald Watt of St Andrews University. Walter Bower, *Scotichronicon*, ed. D.E.R. Watt (9 volumes, Aberdeen 1987–1998). The passage regarding the legend of St Rule is in volume 1 (1993), at pp. 310–17. The passage regarding the foundation of St Andrews University is in volume 8 (1987) at pp. 76–9.

For the University education of Scots prior to 1410, see D.E.R. Watt, *A Biographical Dictionary of Scottish Graduates to AD 1410* (Oxford, 1977).

The Medieval Church of St Andrews, ed. David McRoberts (Glasgow, 1976), provides much useful background to the ecclesiastical pre-eminence of the city.

Chapter 2

Bishop Wardlaw's charter has not survived in the original. Its text, however, is largely recited within the surviving papal bull of 1413.

The petition carried by the Scots mission to the papal curia has not survived in the original. The best guide to the foundation of the University, which details many of the available sources, is James Maitland Anderson, 'The Beginnings of St Andrews University, 1410–1418', in *Scottish Historical Review*, vol. 8, 1910–11, pp. 235–40 and 333–60.

The surviving papal bull of 1413 is held within the University's archives, at reference no. UYUY100.

The remarkable twelfth-century manuscript of works of St Augustine is preserved in the University Library, at reference no. msBR65.A9.

There is a most useful summary of the history of the University Library by Elizabeth Henderson in *Treasures of St Andrews University Library*, ed. Norman H. Reid (London, 2010; hereafter, *Treasures*), which also contains illustrations and essays about the Augustine manuscript, the *Acta Facultatis Artium*, and other items mentioned within the pages of the present work. Further information about the development of the University Library can be found in 'Inventories of Buikis in the Colleges of Sanctandrois, 1588–1612' in *Miscellany* of the Maitland Club (Edinburgh, 1834), vol. 1, pp. 303–29, and M. Simpson, 'St Andrews University Library in the Eighteenth Century: Scottish Education and Print-Culture' (St Andrews University PhD Thesis, 1999). Both *Scottish Libraries*, ed. John Higgitt (Corpus of British Medieval Library Catalogues, vol. 12, London 2006) and John Durkan and Anthony Ross, *Early Scottish Libraries* (Glasgow, 1961) helpfully place the medieval libraries of St Andrews in their broader Scottish context.

I am grateful to Isla Woodman for sight of an unpublished paper which did much to explain the intricacies of the philosophical disputes which characterised the medieval universities.

For further detail of life in the early University, see James Robb, 'Student life in St Andrews before 1450' (*Scottish Historical Review*, 1912, vol. 9, pp. 347–60).

Chapter 3

The papal bull confirming the foundation of St Mary's College is preserved within the University's archives at UYSM110/B1/P1/2.

The purchase of the *birretum* for use at graduation is recorded in the minutes of the University Senatus, on 28 December 1696 (UYUY452/1 f.40v).

The Statutes of St Leonard's College remain in the archives, at UYSL165/2. They are also described within *Treasures*.

Chapter 4

James Melville's Diary was published as *The Diary of Mr James Melvill, 1556–1601* (Bannatyne Club, 1829).

The accounts of Montrose's tutor were published within *Memorials of Montrose*, ed. M. Napier (2 volumes, Maitland Club, 1848–50)

The deed of gift by Alexander Henderson to the University in 1642 is in print: J.B. Salmond and G.H. Bushnell, *Henderson's Benefaction:A Tercentenary Acknowledgment of the University's Debt to Alexander Henderson* (St Andrews, 1942).

Chapter 5

See W.C. Dickinson, *Two Students at St Andrews, 1711–1716* (Edinburgh, 1952).

Thomas Tucker's report is in print: *Upon the Settlement of the Revenues of Excise and Customs in Scotland* (Bannatyne Club, 1825).

The letter of John Row to his uncle is in the Library's manuscript collections at msLF1117.R6. It is also described in *Treasures*.

The material relating to the proposal to move the University to Perth in the 1690s was published in the first (and only) volume of *Transactions of the Literary and Antiquarian Society of Perth* (1827), under the title 'Copies of Papers Relative to a Projected Translation of the University of St Andrews to the City of Perth, in the Years 1697 and 1698'.

Johnson's *Journey to the Western Islands of Scotland* and Boswell's *Journal of a Tour to the Hebrides with Samuel Johnson* are both available in myriad modern editions.

Records of student behaviour in relation to the Jacobite rebellions are to be found in various sources, including the minutes of the Senatus, the College minute books and the minute books of the Burgh of St Andrews (held by the

University Library under the charge and superintendence of the Keeper of the Records of Scotland: series B65/1).

Many of the testimonials supplied to the University on behalf of candidates for medical degrees remain within the archives, at UYUY350.

The poem by Robert Fergusson is quoted from *The Book of St Andrews*, ed. Robert Crawford (Edinburgh, 2005), pp. 41–4 (hereafter referred to as *The Book of St Andrews*).

An undated promotional leaflet for the proposed course in Natural Philosophy is in the archives at UYSS110/AN/9. Its date is deduced from entries in the minutes of the Senatus.

Dempster's letter about education in St Andrews is in the library's manuscript collections at reference ms38422.

The letter from Haldane to Dundas is in the Melville papers, msDA816.D8 (ms4493).

Chapter 6

William Berry's six letters to George Walker are held in the University Library's manuscript collection at msLF1110.B4 (ms37853).

Duncan Dewar's accounts are published: *Duncan Dewar, a Student of St Andrews 100 Years Ago: His Accounts*, ed. Peter Redford Scott Lang (Glasgow, 1926).

The history of Heriot-Watt University and its predecessors is told in *P.N. O'Farrell, Heriot-Watt University – An Illustrated History* (Harlow, 2004).

Information relating to the attempt to elect Sir Walter Scott as Rector is within the Muniments, at reference UYUY223 (Box 1).

The quote regarding Ferrier's work is taken from 'The Philosophy of J. F. Ferrier' by Arthur Thomson, in *Philosophy*, vol. 39, no. 147 (Jan. 1964), pp. 46–62.

The early history of photography is one of the major collection strengths of the University Library. It holds an outstanding collection of the works of John Adamson, Robert Adamson & D.O. Hill, and Thomas Rodger, as well as a large and varied more modern collection, including many photographs of University places and events. A long-standing digitisation project has rendered most of the early photography and an extensive selection of other material available online, which can be accessed via http://www.st-andrews.ac.uk/specialcollections.

The extensive records of the Literary and Philosophical Society of St Andrews are within the University's archives, at UYUY852.

Both the personal library and the personal papers of James David Forbes are now held in the University Library. An avid collector of books, his library contains many rare and important works, especially relevant to the history of science. A brief description is available on the rare books page of the Special Collections website, and the whole collection is catalogued within the library's online book catalogue. His personal papers are equally important, particularly for their fine series of journals and the copious correspondence between Forbes and many of the most eminent scientists and academicians of his day. The collection is fully listed in the online manuscripts catalogue, and has the overall collection reference of msdep7.

Andrew Lang included writing about St Andrews in several works. Best known is his poem *Almae Matres: St Andrews 1862, Oxford 1865*, reprinted in *The Book of St Andrews*, pp. 66–7, and his portrait of the town, *St Andrews*, ed. G. H. Bushnell (St Andrews, 1951). He was also a contributor to the *St Leonard's Magazine*, a handwritten student journal of the 1860s, held in the University library's manuscript collections, at ms30142. The library's extensive holdings of Lang papers and books, which include a bequest made by scholar and biographer of Andrew Lang, Roger Lancelyn Green, are briefly described in *Treasures*.

Margaret Oliphant's story 'The Library Window' is reprinted in *The Book of St Andrews*, pp. 158–201.

The records relating to the proposal to move the University to Dumfries are held within the muniment collections, at UYUY459/A/24, and in the manuscript collections at msDA816.D8.

The records of the LLA scheme are held within the muniment collections at UYUY375–377. There is an article by R.N. Smart describing the scheme: 'Literate ladies – A Fifty Year Experiment', in University of St Andrews *Alumnus Chronicle*, no.59 (June 1968), pp. 21–31.

Further information relating to the founding of University College, Dundee and its development eventually into the University of Dundee can be found in Michael Shafe, *University Education in Dundee, 1881–1981 – A Pictorial History* (Dundee, 1982), and in Donald Southgate, *University Education in Dundee: A Centenary History* (Edinburgh, 1982).

There is a detailed description of the nineteenth-century architectural development of St Andrews in R.D.A. Evetts, 'Architectural Expansion and Redevelopment in St Andrews, 1810–c.1894' (unpublished PhD thesis, University of St Andrews, 1989).

Chapter 7

The public health statistics are taken from John Adamson, *The Sanitary Condition of St Andrews, Compared with that of Other Towns and Country Districts: An Argument for Drainage, Cleansing, and a Better Water Supply* (Cupar, 1862), and from the Fife County Council's Annual Reports on Public Health – contained within the library manuscript collections, in the papers of George Steedman Riddell, ms38099.

Records of the quincentenary celebrations of 1911 are held within the University archives, at UYUY185. I am also grateful to Rachel Hart, Muniments Archivist, for sharing her researches into this subject. The description given in the text relies heavily on her work.

The University's *Rolls of Service* and *Rolls of Honour* for both World Wars are in print, in a single volume for the First World War, printed in 1915, and in separate volumes for the Second World War, printed in 1950.

James Colquhoun Irvine: St Andrews' Second Founder, a biography of Principal Irvine by Julia Melvin, his granddaughter, is due for publication (by John Donald, Edinburgh), in September 2011.

For Willa Muir's writing about St Andrews, see the brief extracts from *Belonging: A Memoir* (Hogarth Press, 1968) included within *The Book of St Andrews*. A major collection of her personal papers are also held in the University Library, at ms38466.

For the role of St Andrews as a centre for cultural renaissance in this period, see Tom Normand, *The Modern Scot: Modernism and Nationalism in Scottish Art, 1928–1955* (Aldershot, 2000).

Chapter 8

Student scrapbooks and reminiscences are a valuable source of information for the modern period. I am grateful to several alumni and members of staff who have been interviewed in the context of an oral history programme in recent years. The comments which have been used in this section have been anonymised to protect their privacy, as has the information which has been derived from a number of personal scrapbooks preserved in the University Library's manuscript collections.

Student newspapers and other publications have been an invaluable source. The pages of *College Echoes*, *Aien*, *The Saint*, *The Alumnus Chronicle*, and, more recently, the *StAndard* (which is available online at http://www.st-andrews. ac.uk/standard/), as well as other newspapers and journals, are a fund of useful information which would never appear in the formal record. These, and the online archive of university press releases at http://www.st-andrews.ac.uk/ news/archive/ are also a rich source of information on academic development, research awards, etc.

The papers of Sir D'Arcy Wentworth Thompson are a major resource for scholarship – a voluminous collection (over 30,000 items) including research papers, annotated monographs and broad-ranging correspondence with many of the greatest minds and most prominent figures of his day. They offer a rich source for the study of the above areas as well as contemporary academia, history, social trends and technological developments. A list of the papers is available on the library's online manuscripts catalogue (ms9013-29950; ms 37781; ms40500-50161).

The records of many of the student societies are preserved within the University's archives at UYUY911.

I am grateful to Peter Adamson for providing information regarding the installation of the first computer in St Andrews. This was written up more fully in P.G. Adamson, 'Professor Stibbs and the First Computer in St Andrews', in the *IT Services Newsletter* (May 2010), available online at http://www.st-andrews.ac.uk/itsold/newsletter/2010/05/stibbs1620.html.

Index

Page references in *italic* refer to illustrations

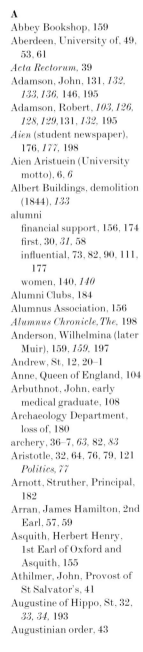

A

Abbey Bookshop, 159
Aberdeen, University of, 49, 53, 61
Acta Rectorum, 39
Adamson, John, 131, *132, 133, 136*, 146, 195
Adamson, Robert, *103, 126, 128, 129*, 131, *132*, 195
Aien (student newspaper), 176, *177*, 198
Aien Aristuein (University motto), 6, *6*
Albert Buildings, demolition (1844), *133*
alumni
    financial support, 156, 174
    first, 30, *31*, 58
    influential, 73, 82, 90, 111, 177
    women, 140, *140*
Alumni Clubs, 184
Alumnus Association, 156
Alumnus Chronicle, The, 198
Anderson, Wilhelmina (later Muir), 159, *159*, 197
Andrew, St, 12, 20–1
Anne, Queen of England, 104
Arbuthnot, John, early medical graduate, 108
Archaeology Department, loss of, 180
archery, 36–7, *63*, 82, *83*
Aristotle, 32, 64, 76, 79, 121
    Politics, 77
Arnott, Struther, Principal, 182
Arran, James Hamilton, 2nd Earl, 57, 59
Asquith, Herbert Henry, 1st Earl of Oxford and Asquith, 155
Athilmer, John, Provost of St Salvator's, 41
Augustine of Hippo, St, 32, *33, 34*, 193
Augustinian order, 43

'Auld Alliance' (1295), 14, 55, 59, 65
Avignon
    papacy, 14, 18, 45–7
    Scots students at, 18

B

Bachelor of Science degree, 141
Bachelor's degree, 35
Balfour of Burleigh, Alexander Hugh Bruce, 6th Lord, as Chancellor, *149*
Barrie, James, as Rector, *153*
Barrow, Reginald, 152
Baxter family, Dundee, 140
Beaton, David, Cardinal Archbishop, 55, 57
Beaton, James, archbishop of St Andrews, 54, 59
Beattie, William, 108
'bejeants', 35, *168*
Bell Pettigrew, James, Professor, *151*
Bell Pettigrew Museum, 150, *151*
Benedict XIII, Pope, *19, 27*
    approval for University, 27–8, 30–1
    bulls (1413), 27, 28, *30*, 30–1, 48
    Scots allegiance to, 18, 45, 47
Berry, Alexander, 118–20, *119*, 121, 122–3, 142, 195
    endowment, 123, 135, 141
birretum, use at graduation, 57, 194
Blackadder, Agnes, *140*, 140, 152
Blackfriars chapel, 32, *32*
Blaeu, Johannes, 90
Bologna, University of, 20
Boer war (1899), 145, 151
Boswell, James, 100–1, 194

Bower, Walter, abbot of Inchcolm Priory, 25, 28, 29, 192
Brewster, David, Principal of United College, 127–8, *128*, 130–1, *131*
Buchanan, George, 67–8, 80
    as Principal of St Leonard's College, 71,
Burghley, David Cecil, Lord, as Rector, *166*
Burns, Robert, 109
Bute, John Crichton-Stuart, 3rd marquis, as Rector, *141, 142*
Bute Medical School, *142*, 152, *161*

C

Calvin, John, 72
Cambridge University, Scots students, 18
Campbell, Adeline, 152
Campbell, Sir Menzies, as Chancellor, *30*, 172, *182, 185*
Cant, Ronald G, 88
    Short History of the University of St Andrews, 9, 191
Carnegie, Andrew, 151
Carnegie, Louise Whitfield, 175
Catholic Church
    influence on government, 47
    medieval education, links with, 20
    reforms, 16th century, 50, 54
    role in society, replacement, 72
    University founded to defend, 26, 50
Celtic Society, 171
Centre for the Study of Terrorism and Political Violence, 184

Chalmers, Thomas, Professor, 125, *126*, 134
Chandos, James Brydges, Duke of, 107, 111
Charles I, King of Scotland and England
  execution, 85, *85*
  opposition to, 84–5, 88
  religious preferences, 83–4
Charles II, King of Scotland and England, 85–6, 92
  in exile, 85, 86
  religious preferences, 85, 86
  restoration, 86, 89
  Scots support, 85–6
Chattan House (1921), 157
Chemistry Society, *173*
Chepman, Walter, printer, 51
class-consciousness, 172–3
cock-fighting, 36
College Echoes (student magazine), *159*, 169, 175, 198
Colleges. *See also* individual Colleges
  amalgamated (1747), 110–11, 112
  autonomy, 60–1, 130
  disputes with faculties, 39, 41, 61
  foundation, 40–3, 54
  renovation, 17th century, 83
  statutes, 61, 97
  student accommodation, 133
  student loyalty to, 64
Commissions, royal and parliamentary, 86–8
  1563, 71
  1579, 71
  1588, 79
  1597, 74
  1690, 96, 97, 99, 116
  1718, 106
  1826, 124, 126, 128
  1840, 128
  1876, 141
  records of, 189–90
'Commonwealth' period, 86, 88, 92
Company of Artillery Volunteers, 151
Confession of Faith, 96, 99
Conjoint Medical School, 108, 160, 162, 173
Constance, Council of (1417), 45, *46*

constitutional reform movement, 123
Cook, George, Professor, 115
Cook, James
  Voyage to the Pacific Ocean, A, *122*
Cook, John I, Professor, 115
Cook, John II, Professor, 115
Cook, John III, Professor, 115
Copyright Act (1709), 120
Cornell, Richard, first teaching staff, 25
Corner, David, 185
Covenanters, 92
Crawford, Robert, 12, 111
Crawford, William Lindsay, 18th Earl, Provost, 96
Cromwell, Oliver, 86, 101
Croyser, William, first teaching staff, 25
Culloden, battle (1746), 104, *104*
Cumberland, William Augustus, Duke of, as Chancellor, 104, 106–7
curriculum
  changes, 18th century, 111–12
  expansion, 19th century, 124–5, 141
  medieval, 18–19
  post-First World War, 156, 160
  regulation (1640s), 87

D
Darien scheme (1690s), 101
David I, King of Scots, 21
David II, King of Scots, 14, 16
Davidson, John, 78
Declaration of Arbroath (1320), 15
degrees
  awarding, 27, 30, 35, 61
  honorary, 150, 184–5
  levels of, 35
Delitae Poetarum Scotorum, 90, *90*
Dempster, George, 113, *113*, 195
determination, 35
Dewar, Duncan, 122, 123, 195
dictates, *75*
Disruption (1843), 125, 134
doctorates, 35
Donaldson, Sir James, Principal, 141, *141*, 148, 150–1, 154–5, 190
Douglas, Gavin, 51, *52*

Douglas, John, Rector of St Mary's College, 77
Dumfries, proposal to move University to, (1814), 135, 196
Dunbar, William, 51
Duncan, Rev George, Professor, 153
Dundee, industrial success, 103, 141
Dundee, John Graham, 1st Viscount, 86
Dundee, University College/ Queen's College, *141*, *143*
  celebrations (1911), 150
  Chair of Botany, 170
  co-education, 140
  College Council, 162
  Conjoint Medical School, 108, 160, 162, 173
  curriculum, technology in, 156
  Dental School, 160
  expansion, 142
  First World War, 152
  foundation, 140, 162
  histories, 196
  Museum of Zoology, *163*
  relationship with University of St Andrews, 140, 160–3
  status, 160–2
  student numbers, 140, 160
Dundee, University of, 163-5, *165*
Dundee Dental Hospital, 160
Dundee War Hospital, 152

E
Edinburgh, University of, 94, 97, 112, 115
education, widening access to, 50, 123–4
Edward II, King, 15
Edward VI, King, 65
Elie, sea trade, *102*
Elizabeth, Queen Mother, *157*, *165*
Elizabeth I, Queen, 67, 68, 76
Elizabeth of Bohemia, 104
England
  Hundred Years' War (1337-1453), 14
  rejects papal authority, 55
  reversion to Catholicism (1550s), 65
  Scotland's relationship with, 14, 15, 16, 18, 55
  Union with (1707), 101, 103

episcopacy
  abolished (1690s), 96
  Stuart preference for, 83, 84, 86, 92
Erasmus, Desiderius, 42, 48, 72, 76
Europe
  medieval nature of, 20
  medieval universities, 192
  nationalism within, 20
  political turmoil, 15
  Reformation, 50
  Scotland's place in, 14
  universities, and Reformation, 72
Ewing, Winnie, *177*
examination, in Latin, 35

F
Faculties
  disputes with colleges, 39, 41, 61
  statutes, revision, 74
Faculty of Arts
  Bursar's Book, 189
  curriculum, 35
  Dean, 39
  deputation to parliament (1430), 48
  discipline, 37
  library, 34
  mace, 39
  Master's degree, 35
  with Medicine, 71
  meetings (1544-51), 58
  minute book, 31, *31*, 52
  presentation gloves, regulation (1460s), 35
  records, 188–9
  rivalry with St Salvator's, 39, 41
  withdraws support from Benedict XIII, 45, *47*
Faculty of Canon Law, mace, *43*
Faculty of Divinity, 71
Faculty of Law, 35, 48, 71
Faculty of Medicine, 35.
  See also Medicine; Conjoint Medical School
Faculty of Science, establishment (1897), 141
Faculty of Theology, 35, 39
Fairlie, Margaret, Professor, 170–1, *171*
Falkland Palace, *49*
Ferguson, Adam, 109
Fergusson, Robert, 109, *109*, 111, *112*

Ferrier, James Frederick, Professor, *130*, 195
  Introduction to the Philosophy of Consciousness, 128
Fife, Robert Stewart, earl of Fife and Duke of Albany, 22, 45
First Book of Discipline, 71
First World War (1914-18), 151–3
Flint, James, Professor, 114
Flint, John, 114
Flodden, battle of (1513), 38, 40
football, 36, 64
Forbes, Donald, 152
Forbes, James David, Principal of United College, 133, 134, *134*, 190, 196
Forsyth, Michael, 177
Fowlis, William, early teacher, 25
Fox-Talbot, William Henry, 131
France
  Hundred Years' War (1337-1453), 14
  and Mary Queen of Scots, 57
  rivalry with Spain, 65
  Scotland's alliance with, 14, 55, 59, 65
franchise, extension, 123
Francis II, King of France, 59, 67–8, 69
Fraser, Simon of Lovat, 106
Freshers' Fair, 172
Freud, Sir Clement, *25, 167*

G
Garrett, Elizabeth (later Anderson), matriculation quashed, 135, 136, *136*
Geddes, Patrick, 170
Geddy, John, map of St Andrews, 6
General Council, 130
George I, King of Great Britain and Ireland, 104
Gill, John, first teaching staff, 25
Gillespie, Alexander, *102*
Glasgow University of, 49, 61, 74, 112, 116
Gledstanes, George, archbishop of St Andrews, 81
Glencoe massacre (1692), 104
'Glorious Revolution' (1688), 86

golf, 12, 37, *64*, 82
Govan, John, first Librarian, 86
Gowdie, John, Principal of Edinburgh University, 115
graduates. *See* alumni
graduation
  'capping' ceremony, 57, 194
  permanent venue, 149, 157
  records, 189
Graham, Thomas, first graduation, 31, *31*
Great Schism (1378–1418), 14, 15, 18, 20, 45, 47
Greek teaching, lack, 79
Green, Andrew, lawyer, 78
Gregory, David, Professor, 109
Gregory, James, Regius Professor, 94, *95,* 97
  Optica Promota, 94, *95*
Grieve, Christopher Murray (Hugh MacDiarmid), 159

H
Haddington, Treaty of (1548), 67
Haig, Field Marshall Douglas, 153, *153*
Haldane, James, Professor, 106
Haldane, Robert, Principal of St Mary's College, 114, *115,* 195
halls of residence, 133, 138, *138,* 169
Hamilton, John, archbishop of St Andrews, 60, 66, 67
  Catechisme, 67
Hamilton, Patrick, trial and execution (1528), 53–4, 58
Harkness, Edward, 157
Hawkwind, 177
Hay, Archibald, Principal of St Mary's College, 54, 59
Hebdomadar, 62
Hebrew teaching, lack, 79
Henderson, Alexander, Leuchars minister, 84, 86, 194
Henry, John, first graduation, 31, *31*
Henry VIII, King of England
  divorce, 56, 68
  and Mary Queen of Scots, 56–7
  rejects papal authority, 55
  'Rough Wooing,' 57, 65
Hepburn, John, prior of St Andrews, 42

heresy trials, 50, 53–4, 57, 58
Heriot-Watt College (later University), 124, 165, 195
Herkless, John, Principal, 155–6
Herring, Percy, Professor, 152
Hewitt, James, 152
higher education, *passim*
  current cutbacks, 186
  expansion, 157, 164
highland clearances, 123
highland society, radical alteration, 106
Hill, David Octavius, *103, 126, 128, 129,* 131, *132,* 195
Hill, Frances, *137*
Hill, George, Principal of St Mary's College, 114, *115,*116
Hill, Henry, Professor, 114
Hill, John, Professor, 114–15, 116
'History of the Universities' project, 9
Hodge, Agnes, 152
Holy Trinity church, 78, 111, 149
Homyll, John, first graduate, 31, *31*
humanist thought, 48, 50–1, 55, 79–80
Hundred Years' War (1337-1453), 14
Hus, John, 72

I
incorporation, 35
industrial revolution, 103, 123
information technology, 183, *184*
International Student Congresses, 175
'Inventoried Papers,' 189
Irvine, Sir James, Principal, 152, *153, 156,* 156–9, 160, 163, 169
  and Dundee, 162
  fundraising, 156, 157

J
Jacobite risings, 104, 105, 106
James, Thomas, degree parchment, *33*
James I, King of Scots, *17,* 47, *47,* 48
  and Church influence, 47
  in English captivity, 17, 20, 22, 23, 45
  Perth as capital, plan, 47
  proposes university move

to Perth, 47–8, 99
  returns to Scotland (1424), 47
  support for University, 28, 47–8
  visits St Andrews, 47
James II, King of Scots, 48
James III, King of Scots, 48
James IV, King of Scots, 48
James V, King of Scots, 48, 55–6
James VI & I, King of Scotland and England, 83
  dispute with Andrew Melville, 74–6, 80
  donates books to University, 81
  and function of University, 74
  as king of England, 76
  liturgy, reform, 84
  visits St Andrews, 80
James VII & II, King of Scotland and England, 86, 96, 104
Jenner, Edward, 108
Johnson, Samuel, 100–1, 103, 112, 194
Johnston, James, St Andrews tailor, 57
John XXII, Pope, 15

K
Kate Kennedy procession, 166, *168*
Kay, John, *117*
Kennedy, James, archbishop of St Andrews, 40, 41–2, *43*
Kerr, Stephen, first graduation, 31, *31*
Kinkell Braes caravan park, *148*
Kinnell, near Forfar, 118
Kinrimund/Kilrymont, 12, 25
Kirk, Reformed
  establishment, 74
  forms of worship, 83–4
  General Assemblies, 84, 86
  prayer book, opposition to, 84
  and public morality, 146
  right of professorial appointments, 87
Knight, William, Professor, *136*
Knox, John, 57, 65–6, *66, 78*
  Elizabeth I alienated by, 68–9
  First Blast of the Trumpet..., 65–6, *66*

and Perth revolt (1559), 68
teaches at University, 76–8
Knox, Sir Thomas Malcolm,
Principal, *164*, 178

L

'Lady Literate in Arts' (LLA)
qualification, 136–8, *137*,
196
Lamberton, William, bishop of
St Andrews, 22
Lang, Andrew, 133, 196
Lang, Brian, Principal, 182,
182
Latin, use of, 35, 63, 80
Lawrence of Lindores, 25, *25*,
39, 47, 50
Lee, John, Principal of United
College, 126–7, *127*
Lennox, Angus, first
graduation, 31, *31*
licence to teach, 35
life expectancy, 17th century,
83
Linguistics Department, loss,
180
literacy, growth of, 50
Litstar, John, first teaching
staff, 25
Livingstone, Thomas, first
graduation, 31, *31*
'Local Examinations,' 138
Luther, Martin, 51, 53, 72

M

McCormick, Joseph, Principal
of United College, 114
MacDiarmid, Hugh, 159
McGillance, Andrew, first
graduation, 31, *31*
MacGregor Mitchell, Robert,
Lord, as Rector, *168*
McIntosh, William
Carmichael, Professor, 157
McIntosh Hall, 157
McIver, Kathleen, 185
Magus Muir, 92
Mair, John, 51, 53
*In quartum sententiarum
quaestiones…, 53*
History of Greater Britain,
51
Malcolm, John, *75*
Marat, Jean Paul, *108*, 109
Marie de Guise, 57
governorship, 59, 65, 66, 67
opposition to, 66, 69
Martin, Ursula, Professor, 171
Martin V, Pope, 45, *46*

martyrs, Protestant, *51*, 53–4,
56, 58
Martyr's Monument, *56*
Mary Queen of Scots, 66, 68, *68*
as heir to English throne, 68
imprisonment and
execution (1587), 69
legacy of books, 80–1
marriage to Francis II, 59,
67–8
returns to Scotland (1561),
69
visits St Andrews, 69
as threat to Protestantism,
56
Mary Tudor, Queen of
England, 56, 65, 66, 67, 68
Master of Arts degree, 125
Master's degree, 35
Mathematics, Chair, 92–4,
111, 112
matriculation, *52*
early, 35
records, 142, 189
women, 135, 142
medicine, 23, 29, 39, 112, 191.
Chair, of, 107, 111, 114
degrees, award of, 108, 125,
195
See also Conjoint Medical
School
Melville, Andrew, Principal of
St Mary's College, *73*,
73–6
dispute with James VI,
74–6, 79, 80
exile in France, 76
flees (1584-5), 79
humanist thought, 79, 80
imprisoned (1606-11), 76
as Principal of St Mary's
College, 73–4, 79, 111
as Rector, 74, 76
Melville, Revd Ephraim, 83
Melville, Henry Dundas, 1st
Viscount, as Chancellor,
114, 115–16, *117*
Melville, James, 76–9, 80,
194
Mercator, Gerard, *Atlas, 15*
Methven, Alexander, first
graduate, 31, *31*
Middleton, Miss Catherine, *30*
Millar, Andrew, printer, 51
Monimail, 58
Montrose, James Graham,
Marquis, 85, 88, 194
execution, 86
as student, 82, *82*, *83*

Montrose, John Graham, 4th
Earl, 76
Moray, Lord James Stewart,
Regent, 69, 81
Muir, Edwin, 159
Muir, Willa (née Anderson),
159, *159*
Belonging: A Memoir, 159,
197
Muniments, University, 188,
190
Murray, Adam, *63*
Music Department, 171, 180

N

'National Covenant,' 84
Natural History, Chair, 170
Nelson Street, *161*
Newton, Isaac, 94
Nimmo, Alexander, 119
'nominalist' school of
philosophy, 18
North Haugh, 163, 178–9, *179*

O

Officer Training Corps, 151
Ogilvie, Henry, 28
Oliphant, John, *100*
Oliphant, Margaret
'Library Window, The,'
134, 196
Opie, John R. A., *92*
Orléans, law school, 17, 18
Oxford, University of, 18, 49

P

papacy
approval for University,
27–8, 30–1
Great Schism (1378–1418),
14, 15, 18, 45, 47
influence, 14–15
power and authority, 18
papal bulls (1413), 27, 28, *30*,
30–1, 190, 193
papal bulls (1538/9), 54, *55*,
193
Paris, University of, 17–18,
18, *21*, 53, 35
parish schooling, post-
Reformation extension,
72–3, 124
parliamentary proceedings,
source, 192
Parliament Hall, 6, *6*, 81, *84*,
86, *87*
Paul III, Pope, 55
Peñiscola, Aragon, 18, 27,
28

Perth
as capital, plan, 47
heresy trial in, 50
parliament held in (1418),
48
parliament held in (1430),
47
revolt (1559), 68
proposal to move university
to (1426), 47–48
proposal to move university
to (1690s), 99–100, 194
Philip II, King of Spain, 65
Philip IV, King of France, 23
philosophy, in medieval
curriculum, 18–19
photography, 131, 195
pier walk, 166, *167*, 186
Pink Floyd, 176, *177*
Pinkie, battle (1547), 59
Pisa, Council of (1409), 18
Pisa, Leaning Tower, *155*
plague, 37–8, *38*, 58, 79, 81
Playfair, Hugh Lyon, Provost,
131, *132*
poetry, first scottish
anthology, 90, *90*
Polish students, 160
Pont, Timothy, 90
prayer book, opposition to, 84
presbyterianism, 83–4
printed books, early, 51
Prior, official visitations, 65
professorships, first woman,
170–1
Protestantism
and humanist thought, 51
martyrs, *51*, 53–4, *56*, 58
Mary Queen of Scots as
threat, 56
opposition to Guise regime,
65
Scotland adopts, 69

R

'Raisin Weekend,' origins, 35,
36, *166*
'realist' school of philosophy,
18
Reformation, 50–8
anti-clericalism, 55
effects, 72, 73
First Book of Discipline, 71
origins, 18
renaissance, 15th century,
48, *49*
Resby, James, 50
Richardson, Louise, Principal,
9, *30*, 184, *185*

Robbins Report (1963), 164
Robert, Bishop of St Andrews, 21, 32
Robert I, King of Scots, 14, 15, 22
Robert II, King of Scots, 16, 22
Robert III, King of Scots, 16, 22, 23
Robert of Montrose, rector of Cults, 40
Rodger, Thomas, *127*, 131, *132*, 195
Ross, Arthur, *105*, 105–6
'Rough Wooing,' 57, 65
Row, John, 97–9, *98*, 194
Roy, James, 152
Royal Scottish Academy of Music and Drama, postgraduate degrees, 180
Rule, St, 12, 25
Rutherford, John, 77
Rutherford, Samuel, Principal of St Mary's College, *88*, 88–9, 92
    Lex Rex, 88, *88, 89*

S
Saint, The (student newspaper), 198
St Andrews, see, 20, 47, 92, 96
St Andrews Castle, 57, 58, *58*
St Andrews Cathedral, 13, 20, *24*, 71
St Andrews Citizen (newspaper), 145, *145*
St Andrews Literary and Philosophical Society, 130–1, *151*, 196
St Andrews Memorial Hospital, *147*
St Andrews Preservation Trust, 192
St Andrews, Priory of
    Faculty of Theology in, 39
    library, 32, *33, 34*
    medieval ownership inscription, 32, *33*
    medieval seal, *23*
    Prior, official visitations by, 65
    and St Leonard's College, 61
St Andrews Prize for the Environment, 184
St Andrews town, *22, 100*
    as burgh, 21–2
    Burgh minute books, 194
    as centre of Scottish church, 20–2, 50, 80, 101
    child mortality, 146
    climate, 12
    death rate (1900), 146
    decline, 18th century, 101–3
    earliest book printed, 67, *67*
    expansion, 141, 146, 180
    golf course, *13*
    harbour, *103*
    histories, 191–2
    hub of Scottish cultural identity (1930s), 159, 197
    investment post-Restoration, 92
    location, 12
    Market Street, 22
    medieval importance, 21–2
    New Year celebration, 145
    North Street, *3*, 40, 45, 53, *54, 131*, 149
    parish church, 71, 111
    parliament held in (1309), 22–3
    parliament held in (1645–6), 81
    photographers, early, 131
    plan, 22
    population, 13–14, 146
    prosperity, 19th century, 141–2, 197
    public health, 99, 146, 197
    and Reformation (1570s), 71
    in 'Rough Wooing,' 57
    as royal seat, 12
    royal visits, 48, 69, 80
    sanitation, 146
    The Scores, *143*
    Second World War, *161*
    size, 13–14
    street lighting, 146
    South Street, 22, 31–2, 40, 45, *84*, 86
    tourism, *147*
    University, relationship with, 26, 45, 64–5, 79, 96–7, 99–100, 135, 141–2, 156
St Andrews, University of.
    See also Colleges; Commissions; curriculum; Faculties; graduation; matriculation; Senatus; students; teaching staff; University Calendar
    academic standards, 71
    building programme (1890s), 141, 142
    central control, lack, 71
    central teaching accommodation, 40
    as centre of religious and political life, 20, 70, 80
    Chancellor
        archbishop as, 80
        election, 87
        role, 38–9, 61, 130
    charter of incorporation (1412), 26, 27
    coat of arms, 28
    Commonwealth period, 92
    competition from Scottish universities, 103
    decline
        16th century, 72, 79
        18th century, 101, 109–10, 112, 116
        19th century, 134–5
    distance learning, 136–7
    Dundee, relationship with, 140, 160–3
    as early community, 31
    egalitarianism, 49
    expansion, 178, 179–80
    as federation of colleges, 60–1, 64
    financial difficulties, 106, 134, 135, 137, 141, 180–1
    first computer, 183, *183*, 198
    First World War (1914-18), 151–3, 197
    foundation (1410-11), 13–14, 17, 20, 22–3, 26–31, *27*, 28, *30*, 30–1, 193
    founding ideals, 26, 50
    function, 74
    fundraising, 149, 156
    governing structure, 19th century reform, 128–30
    government funding, 174, 175
    internal disputes, 39–40, 135
    international politics, role, 45, 47
    Jacobitism, 105–6, 107, 194
    James I, association with, 47, *47*
    Library, 118
        catalogues, 120, *120*, 121
        collections, 81
        Copyright Act and, 120
        foundation, 32–4, 80–1
        growth, 120, 121
        history, 193
        importance, 34
        King James Library, 6, *6*, 81, *81, 84*, 86
        North Street site, 178, 179, *180*
        records of, 190–1
        South Street site, 86, 121, *121*
        Special Collections Department, 188
    links with Cathedral and Priory, 32
    and loss of archbishopric, 92
    maces, *25*, 39, *39*, 42, *43*, 48, 58
    as major theological centre, 80
    medieval organisation, 38–9
    medieval seal, *33*
    motto, 6, *6*
    muniments (archives), 9, 61, 188–91
    Museum of, *63*
    and National Covenant, 84–5, 86
    as national university, 45, 61
    nepotism, 114–16
    'New Foundation' (1579), 71, 72
    organisation, medieval, 26, 31–2, 38–9
    pedagogy, 40, 47, 54, 60
    Principals. *See also* Arnott; Donaldson, Irvine, Herkless, Knox, Lang; Richardson; Watson
        first woman, 184, *185*
        official residence, 141
        records of, 190
        role, 39
    pro-episcopalianism, 105
    property, 39–40
    quincentenary (1911), 148–51, *149, 150*, 197
    Rector
        authority over Colleges, 71
        duties, 26
        election, 39, 86, 125–6, 128–30, 175
        first, 39
        official visitations, 65

St Andrews, University of
(contd.)
power, 26, 74
role, 39, 61
term of office, 39, 76
and Reformation, 50–8,
70–1, 72
regents, regenting system,
60, 64, 74, 87, 111
relocation proposals, 47,
48, 99–100, 135,
194,196
reorganisation
16th century, 71
1640s, 86–8, 94
1747, 110, 111–13
19th century, 128–30
research activity, 184, 185
Second World War
(1939–45), 160, 161, 197
sexcentenary, 9, 186
size, 49, 82
suffragette action, 139
theological and political
controversy, 53–4
town, relationship with, 26,
45, 79, 135, 141–2, 156
Vice-Chancellor, 39, 80
withdraws support from
Benedict XIII, 45, 47
women's education,
135–40
St John's College, 40, 48, 81, 81
St Leonard, Hospital of, 31-2,
43
St Leonard's College, 32, 44
alumni, 90
attached to Priory, 42–3
chapel, 43, 44, 111
endowments, 42–3, 90
fire (1702), 106
'foundation bible'(?), 45
histories, 191
humanities focus, 71, 90
inter-college rivalry, 64
Jacobitism within, 105, 106
lectures on dialectic, 75
library, 81
minute books, 189
sold, 111
Statutes, 61–5, 62, 194
student life, 61–5, 97–9
united (1747), 110, 111,
112–13
visitations by Prior, 65
St Leonard's Hall, 133
St Leonard's Magazine, 196
St Leonard's Parish Church,
111

St Mary of the Rock church, 13
St Mary's College, 60
and amalgamation (1747),
110
early difficulties, 59
fire (1727), 106
first Principal, 73–4
foundation, 40, 54, 55, 59,
193
histories, 191
minute books, 189
official visitations, 65
organisation, 60
professorial appointments,
87
re-founding (1550s), 60, 66
statutes, 61
syllabus, 60
teachers, 77
teaching methods, 74
as theological college, 54, 60,
71, 134
St Salvator's College, 41, 77,
129, 174
autonomy, 40–1
chapel, 41, 42, 42, 43, 47,
133, 157
charter, 40
creation, 40
histories, 191
humanities focus, 71
inter-college rivalry, 64
mace, 42, 43
organisation, 40
PH monogram, 53–4, 54
rebuilding post-
Restoration, 92
Rectorial visitations, 65
relationship with
University, 40–1
rivalry with Faculty of
Arts, 39, 41
size, 110
statutes, 61
tower attacked (1547),
58, 59
united (1747), 110, 111,
112–13
St Salvator's Hall, 157, 158
Salmond, Alex, 177, 178
Scheves, John, first teaching
staff, 25
scholastic philosophy, 80
School of Arts of Edinburgh
(later Watt Institution/
Heriot-Watt College/
University), 124
Scot, John, of Scotstarvit,
90, 91

Scotland
allegiance to Avignon
papacy, 18, 45–7
alliance with France, 14,
55, 59, 65
Catholic regime, and
reform, 66
Commonwealth period, 86
demographic change, 123
divided allegiances, 59
east coast burghs decline,
101
England, relationship
with, 14, 15, 16, 18, 55
first printed books, 51
histories, 192
industrialisation, 103
Jacobite cause, 104,
105–6
place in Europe, 14
political and economic
disarray, 14th century,
16–17
political turmoil, 17th
century, 83–6, 92, 94,
96, 103
pro-Catholic party, 57
Protestantism, official
adoption, 69
Protestant martyrs, 51,
53–4, 56, 58
rule by regents (1406-
24), 17
sea trade, 101
as 'special daughter' of
Catholic Church, 20
traditional eastern trade,
15, 102
Union (1707), 101, 103
wars of independence, 16
Scotstarvit estate, 90, 91
Scott, Francis George, 159
Scott, Sir Walter, 125–6, 195
Scottish Chamber Orchestra,
180
Scottish Enlightenment, 112
scriptorium, 23
Scrymgeour, Alexander,
Professor, 106
Second World War (1939–45),
160, 161
Senatus Academicus, 105, 114,
135, 153
foundation, 87
minutes, 154, 189, 194
power, 130
Sharp, James, archbishop of
St Andrews, 92, 93
Short, James, 95

Simson, Thomas, Professor,
107
Skene, Alexander, as Rector, 96
Smith, Alexander, Principal's
servant, 78
Smith, Robert, first graduate,
31, 31
Somerset, Edward Seymour,
'Protector,' 59
South Africa, Anglo-Boer war
(1899), 145, 151
Spain, rivalry with France, 65
'Sports Hall of Fame,' 172
St Andard, The, staff
magazine, 186, 198
Stephenson, William, first
teaching staff, 25
Stewart, Alexander, archbishop
of St Andrews, 40
Stewart, James Francis
(James VIII) ('the Old
Pretender'), 104
Stewart monarchy, support
for, 104
Stibbs, Walter, Professor, 183
Stirling, University of, 165
Strathclyde University, 165
Student Association, 171–2,
176, 177
student life
early days, 34–7, 193
16th century, 61–5, 76–9
17th century, 97–9
19th century, 125
1930s, 172
1960s, 176–7
women, 169
student newspapers, 198
Student Representative
Council, 142
students
accommodation, 116, 133,
138, 142, 157, 168, 169
age, 61
attainment, levels, 35
college duties, 62
diet, 63, 142
discipline, 36–7, 37, 64
dress, 36, 63, 64
fees, 82
first, 31, 31
First World War, 151, 152
inter-college rivalry, 64
lecture notes, 75
military training, 151
'minus potens,' 83
non-graduating, 109
numbers
medieval, 49

students (*contd.*)
    18th century, 101, 109, 110
    19th century, 134–5, 139
    20th century, 148, 151,
      156, 160, 174, 178, 180
    from overseas, 174–5, 180
    pastimes, 36–7, 63, 64, 78, 82
    Polish, 160
    'potens', 83
    poverty, 40, 48–9, 61, 83,
      124
    privileges, 26, 27, 30, 47
    reading habits, 121–2
    records, 189
    Scottish, 173
    social class, 83, 124, 172–3
    societies, 171–2, *173*
    studies, 62
    study overseas, 17–18
    traditions, 166, *167, 186*
    on University committees,
      175–6
    war service, 152
    weapons, use, 64, 96
    women, 135–40, *140*, 159
Students' Representative
  Council (SRC), 175
Students' Union, 175, 176,
  176, 177, 179
students' union building, 142
suffragettes, 139, *139*
Sutherland, John Gordon,
  14th Earl, *82*

T
'Tables' committee (1638), 84
taxation, freedom from, 26,
  27, 30, 48
teaching methods, 34–5, 74
teaching staff, 184
  attractions for, 186–7
  disputes with Faculty,
    39–40
  early, 25
  expansion, 142, 148
  John Knox, 76–8
  oath of allegiance, 96
  regents, 64, 74, 77, 97, 99,
    111
  salaries, 116
technical education, 124
Tedder Commission (1952),
  162
Theological Society, 171
Wentworth Thompson, Sir
  D'Arcy, Professor, 156,
  163, 169, 169–70, 190
  On Growth and Form,
    169–70, *170*

papers, 197
Thorpe Davie, Cedric, Master
  of Music, 171, 180
Tucker, Thomas, 92, 101, *103,*
  194
Tullibardine, John Murray,
  Earl of, as Chancellor, 99
Tullidelph, Thomas, Principal
  of St Leonard's College, 109,
  110, *110,* 111
Tulloch, John, senior
  Principal, 134
Tunnock's Caramel Wafer
  Appreciation Society, *172*
Tynninghame, Andrew, first
  graduation, 31, *31*

U
Union, Parliamentary (1707),
  101, 103
United College of St Salvator
  and St Leonard in the
  University of St Andrews
  curriculum, 111–12
  formation, 110–11
  minute books, 189
  professorial
    establishment, 111
  rebuilding (1830s), 128,
    129, 133
universities
  local provision, 20
  medieval, 13–14, 17–19,
    20, 72
  new (1960s), 164–5
  post-Reformation, 73
  technological, 164
Universities (Scotland) Acts
  1840, 128, 130
  1889, 140, 174, 175
  1966, 178
University Calendars, *125,*
  137, 190
University Court, 128–30,
  141, 154
University Hall, 138, *138,* 169
University of St Andrews Act
  (1953), 162

V
Valois, house of, 68
Vesalius, Andrew
  De Humani Corporis
    Fabrica, 107
Walker, George, 118, *119,* 120,
  121, 123, 142, 195
Wardlaw, Henry, bishop of St
  Andrews, 23–5, 30
  charter of incorporation

(1412), 26, 27, 31, 193
  coat of arms, 25
  founding ideals, 50
  gifts to University, 40, 48
Watson, John Steven,
  Principal, 178, 180–2
Watson, Robert, Professor,
  100, 109, 111
Watt Institution (later Heriot-
  Watt College/University),
  Edinburgh, 124, 137–8, 139
Westminster Confession of
  Faith, 89
Whyte, James, 159
Wilkie, James, Principal of St
  Leonard's College, 78
Wilkie, Robert, Principal of St
  Mary's College, *45*
Wilkie, William, Professor,
  109
William III & Mary II, joint
  monarchy of England and
  Scotland, 86, 96, 104
William of Wales, Prince, *30*
Wilson, James, 109, *109*
Wishart, George, execution,
  51, 57, 65
Wode, Thomas, vicar of St
  Andrews, *59*
women
  banned, 63, 135
  distance learning, 136–7
  early matriculation, 138
  education, demand for, 137
  first Principal, 184, *185*
  halls of residence, 138, *138,*
    157, 169
  higher education, 135–40
  Lady Literate in Arts
    qualification, 136–8, *137,*
    196
  matriculation, 135, 142
  medical students, 152
  professorships, 170–1
  Students' Union, 175
  suffrage, 135, 137, 139, *139*
Wycliffe, John, 50, 72

Y
Yellowlock, William, first
  graduation, 31, *31*
Younger, George, 1st
  Viscount, 157
Younger, Sir James, *153*
Younger Hall, 149, 157, *157,*
  180

Z
Zwingli, Huldreich, 72